Oishii!

Oishii!

JAPANESE FOOD STYLE

Manami Okazaki

Prestel
Munich • London • New York

CONTENTS

Japanese Food Traditions

Contemporary Cuisine

Pop Culture and Design

Working with Food

ART

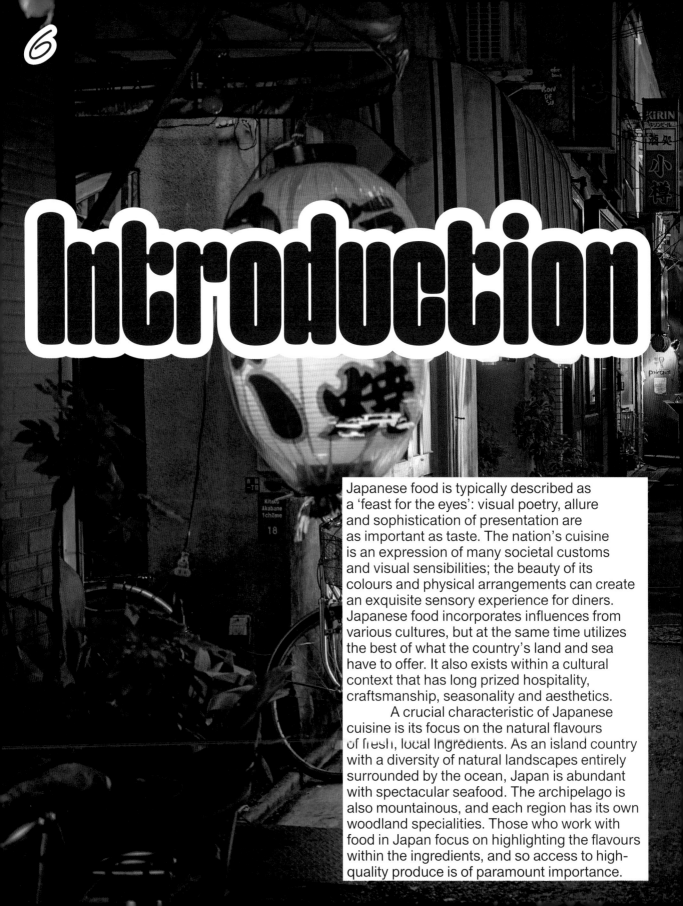

Introduction

Japanese food is typically described as a 'feast for the eyes': visual poetry, allure and sophistication of presentation are as important as taste. The nation's cuisine is an expression of many societal customs and visual sensibilities; the beauty of its colours and physical arrangements can create an exquisite sensory experience for diners. Japanese food incorporates influences from various cultures, but at the same time utilizes the best of what the country's land and sea have to offer. It also exists within a cultural context that has long prized hospitality, craftsmanship, seasonality and aesthetics.

A crucial characteristic of Japanese cuisine is its focus on the natural flavours of fresh, local ingredients. As an island country with a diversity of natural landscapes entirely surrounded by the ocean, Japan is abundant with spectacular seafood. The archipelago is also mountainous, and each region has its own woodland specialities. Those who work with food in Japan focus on highlighting the flavours within the ingredients, and so access to high-quality produce is of paramount importance.

Japanese restaurant culture began to flourish during the Edo era. Nowadays, Tokyo is filled with small eateries.

While Tokyo is known for high-end gastronomy, the city is rife with unpretentious, intimate restaurants where locals dine.

A late-night soba store. Eateries like this are a common sight in Japanese cities.

In Japan, food is seen as an way to visually showcase nature: to incorporate the inherent beauty of its gifts, and to express seasonality and the shifts between the four seasons. Everything, from the ingredients to the garnishes, from flowers to tableware, celebrates summer, autumn, winter and spring. Naturally, seasonal differences between various regions result in a wide range of food. For example, the tropics of Okinawa boast cuisine unlike that of the frigid, snowy landscapes of Northern Honshu and Hokkaido, where intense cold necessitates preservation methods not found in other parts of Japan. Many of these techniques, such as fermentation, are based on folk wisdom passed down through the generations.

Temari (hand ball) sushi from Aoki, considered to be the best in Tokyo.

Japanese food is as much about procuring excellent produce as it is about cooking.

Sakuma Drops are a type of hard candy that made an iconic appearance in the heart-breaking anime film *Grave of the Fireflies* (1988), directed by Isao Takahata.

Celebratory meals such as *osechi*, eaten at New Year's, are important aspects of Japanese food culture.

As a result of Japan's reverence for the seasons, festive days are celebrated in ways that also relate to the country's food culture. Special dishes called *gyoji-shoku* are eaten only during certain events, and because of this, there is an awareness about what ingredients are in season – even among laypeople. Typical celebratory foods for New Year's include *osechi-ryori*, a mix of dishes, and freshly pounded *mochi* (sticky rice). For *Hinamatsuri* (Doll's Day) on 3 March, *hamaguri* clam soup is served, and on Children's Day, 5 May, *chimaki* rice balls are prepared in a leaf, and so on.

When discussing Japanese food aesthetics, it is necessary to look at the cultural context in which the cuisine is consumed. The nation's visual ideals are heavily influenced by Buddhism, in particular Zen Buddhism. *Yugen*, a concept that guides Japanese sensibilities, is usually translated as 'mysterious profundity'. It refers to an object's nuances and subtleties beyond what is obvious and plainly stated. *Yugen* is focused on our human realm and the experiences that exist within it, rather than imaginary worlds. Besides what is observable in the literal sense, it describes what is implied or suggested – the latent beauty of things. Creating summer dishes that look like water and are hence cooling to the eyes is one example of how the concept of *yugen* can be used in food.

Within Buddhism, the idea of nothingness also holds great significance. Everything is thought to come from, and go back to, oblivion. As such, food presentation isn't focused on volume; empty space is a key element utilized in an elegant manner.

Wabi-sabi is a concept influenced by Zen Buddhist philosophies too, and describes the beauty inherent within imperfections and flaws. It is concerned with appreciating the transitory essence of life, impermanence and the cyclical characteristics of nature. *Wabi-sabi* espouses an acceptance of nature, rather than a will to dominate or overcome it. As such, imbalance and an understated earthiness are seen to be beautiful (for example, falling petals after cherry blossoms bloom). These sensibilities guide Japan's artisanal aesthetic, which champions humble beauty, rather than the type of perfection that can be achieved through mass production.

There are several key elements to consider in thinking about how Japanese food looks, such as the use of ingredients, colours, cutting skills and tableware. Rather than the stark white dishes one might expect in Western restaurants, for example, Japanese eateries often use a menagerie of vessels of various sizes, shapes and hues. Each is chosen carefully to complement a meal and the dishes are never arranged symmetrically, as that is seen as forced and unnatural.

The dish known as *hassun*, which is part of the standard set of courses called *kaiseki* served at refined Japanese-style restaurants known as *ryotei*, is among the most aesthetically pleasing. It is made up of an array of delights offered on a 24 cm (9.5 in.) tray, the presentation of which is bound by a set of rules. There is holistic consideration given to where the food is placed: chopsticks are laid out in front of the tray, while delicacies from the sea and the mountains are presented on the upper right and lower left, respectively.

The notion that eating is a sensory experience revolving around much more than taste is not culturally specific to Japan, and has long been exploited on an industrial level. As scholar Ai Hisano, a Senior Lecturer at the Graduate School of Economics at Kyoto University – who has extensively researched the visualization of taste – has discovered, sensory information such as colour (the yellow of margarine, the bright redness of meat, and so on) is something that has been emphasized by food businesses since the late nineteenth century.

The saying that Japanese cuisine is a 'feast for the eyes' is a reflection of how much its visual qualities are taken into consideration when creating food. From the tableware to the arrangement, every detail is intended to result in dishes that are nothing short of an artistic achievement. This book aims to show the manifold ways food is celebrated as an aesthetic experience. From cute sweets and parfaits to the most sophisticated haute cuisine, Japan is a culture where food is an optical delight, designed to titillate the eyes as much as the taste buds.

Shigeru Kato hunts boar with ancient breeds of Japanese dogs such as the Kishu and Shikoku. Hunting with dogs is one of Japan's oldest food-related traditions.

Cat *onigiri* (rice balls) from Kuronekosha Café in Tokyo. *Kawaii* (cuteness) is one of the most influential aesthetic values that dictates the appearance of food.

Food and spirituality are inextricably linked in Japan. This fire festival in Nozawa acts as a prayer to promote a good harvest.

A COOKING CULTURE OF FIVES
The most important elements within Japanese food are said to be the five senses, the five colours, the five cooking methods and the five flavours. Paying attention to these creates a harmonious and balanced meal, while giving diners a wonderful experience.

All of Japan's traditional cooking techniques can be experienced during a *kaiseki* meal, such as this one at Sakan Shoan, Matsushima Bay, Miyagi.

Five senses
Of course, the five senses – sight, hearing, smell, touch and taste – are of vital importance in Japanese cuisine. They determine whether food can be considered delicious, and cement the notion that it is not something merely to be tasted.

Five colours
Traditional Japanese cuisine is primarily comprised of five colours: white, blue/green, yellow, red and black. They are viewed as harmonious, and have been a feature of the nation's food since Buddhism flourished during the Nara era (710–794). It is thought that emphasizing colour in the arrangement of foods, such as adding black sesame to red pickled plums, will lead to a dish that is healthy and balanced. The warming colours, like red and yellow, are seen as stimulating, while the cooling colours are refreshing.

Kaiseki is the most sophisticated of Japan's traditional meals.

Five cooking methods
Japanese cooking is comprised of five methods: *nama* (cutting), *niru* (simmering), *yaku* (grilling), *ageru* (frying) and *musu* (steaming). In a traditional multi-course *kaiseki* meal, it is possible to enjoy all of these methods. *Kaiseki* meals usually start with gentle flavours, followed by subtle simmered vegetables. As the courses progress, there will be tempura, grilled fish and meat. The meal then goes down in intensity, finishing with rice, soup and condiments.

One of the characteristics that defines Japanese food is the use of sophisticated cutting techniques. Artisanal knife skills are key, and for some foods, slicing is the main form of preparation as many ingredients are eaten raw. During the Edo period, the notion that the most refined foods require the least amount of cooking prevailed, in order to highlight natural ingredients. Indeed, witnessing the slicing of sashimi is a sight to behold, as a chef masterfully slivers a fish with controlled strokes to reveal exquisite colours and textures. Knife skills are also necessary to make shapes with garnishes, such as vegetables, in the likeness of motifs that evoke the seasons.

Simmering is a technique whereby ingredients are placed into stock, and by heating them, their textures become softer. Steaming is also very common. Grilling usually takes the form of ingredients being exposed directly to a flame, and frying is a method used to cook food in a short amount of time while retaining its flavour.

Five flavours
The five flavours that make up Japanese cuisine are sweetness, sourness, saltiness, bitterness and *umami*. While the first four are part of the global lexicon, much of the rest of the world has adopted the Japanese term *umami*. It refers to a flavour profile that includes glutamic acid, and is the core taste of *dashi* broth. It is typically extracted from *konbu* seaweed, bonito, dried shiitake and shellfish.

Seasons

Rice

Festivals

Gift-Giving

History

Wagashi

Japanese Food Traditions

History

Ryuryukyo Shinsai, *Sushi and New Year's Sake*, c. Edo period (1615–1868), woodblock print; ink and colour on paper.

There have been a number of large changes within Japanese food culture that have shaped what it's like today. One of the most cataclysmic of these was the introduction of rice paddy agriculture in the Yayoi period (300 BCE to 300 CE), which led to rice becoming the staple food of the nation. Particularly since the sixth century there was also rampant importation of Chinese culture, which impacted every aspect of Japanese society. However, as Japan was not a Chinese colony, elements were not imported wholesale but were cherry-picked and then localized.

Utagawa Hiroshige, *Crayfish and Two Shrimps*, *c*. 1840, woodblock print; ink and colour on paper.

Utagawa Toyokuni, 1802–03, woodblock print; ink and colour on paper. Part of a triptych depicting famous *kabuki* actors in the dressing room of an Edo theatre. One is holding a wine glass, and the others are eating a hotpot and sushi.

EDO-ERA WOODBLOCK PRINTS

The Edo era is when most traditional Japanese dishes were developed. *Ukiyo-e* woodblock prints created at the time served not only as art, but as a form of popular media depicting daily scenes and rituals, theatre actors and courtesans (who were celebrities to the commoner class), and domestic life. Artists such as Utamaro made portraits of beautiful women engaging in everyday activities like cooking. These types of household scenes show in detail the way food was prepared, for example the method of *kabayaki*, which is used to grill and steam eel. Woodblock scenes often depict not only ingredients, but also the procurement of food, such as fishing scenes, preparation and vendors.

Some prints also depict the dishes that were considered celebratory, as well as the foods that were eaten at festivals and theatre outings. It is clear from these prints that the enjoyment of food was considered a form of pleasure, and a lifestyle that had a high sensitivity to the seasons and locality.

Utagawa Hiroshige, *The Aoyagi in Ryogoku*, c. 1835–42, woodblock print; ink and colour on paper. This piece is part of a series depicting Edo's famous gastronomic landmarks.

Buddhism first entered Japan from China, via Korea. This led to bans on the consumption of meat, based on the Buddhist doctrine that sees all living things as equal and disavows the killing of animals for food. The first Japanese law banning meat was put in place in 675. With the establishment of Buddhism as the state religion, there was mass promulgation of meat bans, which were enacted numerous times over the course of several centuries. Because of this, livestock-based farming did not become the norm until modern times. This resulted in a diet that was heavily reliant on seafood, vegetables and soy products, which has made Japanese cuisine incredibly healthy due to its lack of animal fats.

From the sixteenth to the seventeenth century, Japan also received inspiration from ingredients that came originally from neighbouring countries, most of which arrived on Portuguese trade ships. These included items that are now part of the lexicon of Japanese food but were exotic at the time, such as pumpkin, sweet potato and chilli. Sugar also started to play a larger role and began to be farmed in Okinawa in 1623. Another influential technology that entered from Thailand was distillation.

Hashimoto Chikanobu, *Moon-Viewing Party,* from the series *The Inner Precincts at Chiyoda*, 1898, woodblock print; ink and colour on paper. Part of a triptych depicting a young woman of samurai rank viewing the full moon (in another panel), with ladies-in-waiting carrying food.

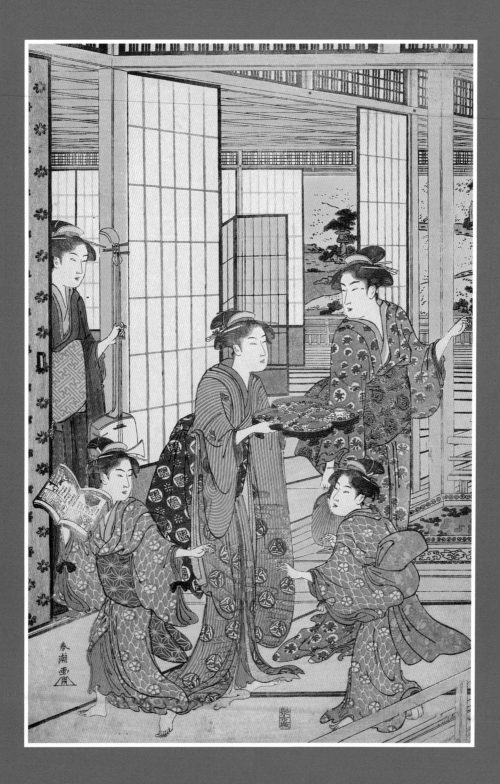

Katsukawa Shuncho, *A Young Woman with a Tray of Sweetmeats, c.* 1780–95, woodblock print; ink and colour on paper.

In the Edo period (1603–1868), Japan's borders were closed (except to a limited number of Dutch and Chinese trade ships that entered via the port of Nagasaki). As such, the country embraced an isolationist policy, during which time traditional Japanese food was able to develop its own identity. Many aspects of the nation's cooking that were established in the Edo era formed the basis of what we know as Japanese food today, such as soba, tempura, eel and sushi. The Edo era also saw the popularization of *dashi* broth based on bonito and kelp, as well as the use of soy sauce. Techniques that were once highly guarded became widely known as cookbook publishing flourished. Moreover, because it was a time of peace, much of the mercantile class had disposable income and the concept of dining for pleasure started to thrive. Many eating establishments sprang up.

The Meiji period (1868–1912) saw another major transformation in Japanese food culture as the country developed into a modern nation state. Borders opened, and there was a sudden shift towards industrialization and internationalization. These overarching societal changes saw the nation's cuisine become increasingly Westernized. The consumption of meat started to be encouraged, as the government thought that people were lacking in physical strength compared to Westerners due to their diets. Initially, Western food was a luxury that was accessible only to elites, but it gradually spread to the masses. However, as it became more standard within Japan, an amalgamation of Japanese and Western food occurred, leading to fusion dishes such as *kare-rice* (curry rice; see page 70 for cafés that serve the best of these localized dishes).

After World War II, Japan was devastated and starvation was rampant, so its main focus became increasing food production. As the country's economy began rapidly to grow, appliances such as fridges and gas cookers changed the way food was stored and prepared.

In more recent years, Japanese cuisine has flourished, becoming one of the most highly lauded in the world. There is an insatiable passion for eating as well as cooking in Japan. Much of the country's popular culture and media is devoted to food, from competition-style cookoffs to travel shows to creative cooking showcases. Turn on the TV at any given hour and there will be a show about cooking, or hosts simply gobbling delicacies, followed by hyperbolic exclamations of *Oishii!* ('Delicious!'). In 2013, UNESCO awarded *washoku* (Japanese cuisine) Intangible Cultural Heritage status. The Michelin guide for 2023 awarded Tokyo the most stars of any city in the world, an honour it has held for a few years running. Kyoto and Osaka are also home to almost 200 Michelin-starred restaurants each.

Japanese food is – and always has been – overwhelmingly the outcome of influence from other cultures. A combination of wisdom, technique, produce and aesthetic sensibility has resulted in one of the most loved cuisines on the planet.

Kitagawa Utamaro, *Kitchen Scene*, c. 1794–95, woodblock print; ink and colour on paper.

Seasons

Sakura viewing while picnicking is a popular spring pastime in Japan.

Japan is a culture predicated on the four clearly defined seasons of spring, summer, autumn and winter. Traditional aesthetic sensibilities and artistic reflections are centred on the changing of these distinct periods; the nation's cultural proclivity towards seasonality is expressed visually, and not only through taste.

Fine dining in Japan is founded on the notion that a meal is only successful if the essence and innate qualities of the ingredients themselves are able to shine. The practice of using seasonal ingredients when they are at their most delicious and fresh is referred to as *shun*.

Chefs may also choose the sophisticated method of using *hashiri* (early harvest) and *nagori* (last harvest) produce. They maintain relationships with vendors at markets, farms and fisheries in order to obtain the finest ingredients, since the enjoyment of seasonal foods is highly anticipated and viewed as one of the main pleasures within Japanese cuisine culture. While produce can technically be imported or grown in indoor environments, so ingrained is the notion of seasons that certain foods are deemed inappropriate to eat outside of their optimum timeframe.

Evidence of sensitivity to and appreciation for seasonality in all facets of culture, including poetry and art, goes back as far as the Heian period (794–1185). The celebration of seasons was an intrinsic part of tea ceremony culture, brought to Japan by Zen monks who studied in China. During the Edo era, the notion that participating in the first catch of the season or the first harvest would ensure longevity and good luck led to the formation of rituals that are celebrated to this day. Even now, consumers will pay exorbitant fees to procure what are ostensibly the first melons of a harvest, or the first tuna catch.

Attention to seasonality is seen within every aspect of both traditional and contemporary Japanese food culture. The entire aesthetic experience, from colour palette to tableware to the flowers and leaves used for garnishing, completely changes, whether it's a classic multicourse *kaiseki* meal (see page 132), *wagashi* sweets (see page 44) or festival foods (see page 42). For instance, earthy bowls are used in autumn, while summer tableware often employs glass to evoke a sense of coolness. Contemporary food is equally beholden to the seasons, with many snack companies and fast food chains releasing limited-edition themed products.

Symbolically, spring is a time of change and rebirth. It marks the new school and business years and heralds the end of winter. Everything has a jubilant, magical atmosphere, and people in Japan seem more relaxed as the weather warms. Spring is intrinsically linked to cherry blossoms (*sakura*), the resplendent pink flowers that explode during the season. *Hanami*, or the tradition of viewing *sakura* while enjoying bento lunch boxes that are either home-prepared or purchased at stores, along with copious amounts of alcohol, is a national pastime.

Spring vegetables include snow *fuki* (a stalk vegetable), *takenoko* (bamboo shoots), peas, spring cabbage, rape blossom and onions. Other spring foods include clams, *shirasu* (whitebait), cuttlefish and herring (hence seafood soups are popular). Sweet foods include *ichigo daifuku*, a sticky rice cake with a strawberry placed inside with red bean paste. Another iconic sweet is the confectionary company Toraya's *'sakura-no-sato' yokan*. In spring, every type of sweet food seems to takes a pink tone and typically uses strawberry or cherry-blossom themes. Starbucks produces *sakura* cherry Frappuccinos; chocolatier Godiva makes *sakura*-themed white chocolate drinks; there are pink KitKats, *sakura* macarons, Pockys, parfaits, ice cream and afternoon tea sets in Tokyo hotels.

Spring is the time to enjoy an array of gorgeous traditional sweets.

SPRING

Summer

Somen noodles on a glass plate. During summer, clear 'cooling' materials such as glass are used as tableware.

Japanese summers are sweltering, humid affairs that require a lot of stamina to endure. After a long, rainy monsoon season that starts in June and can last for weeks, the onset of summer brings brutally hot days. People crave refreshing dishes, or food they believe will bring them stamina. It is also the season for intense and explosive festivals (see page 34) and fireworks displays, at which attendees dress in *yukata* (cotton summer kimonos). Summer delicacies are often visually 'cooling', for example utilizing goldfish motifs, or jelly-like translucent foods that appear watery.

Typical summer ingredients include cucumber, bitter melon and aubergine (eggplant). Popular dishes include thin *somen* (noodles), which are served cold with a dipping sauce, and *chuka* ramen, a cold ramen dish with various toppings such as egg, cucumber and tomato. *Unagi* (eel) is also popular, as it is believed it will provide energy in the heat. Iconic sweet summer foods include watermelon, cherries, various citrus fruits, peaches and grapes. *Kakigori* (shaved ice) is a beloved summer snack.

Autumn

Matsutake are luxurious, aroma-rich mushrooms that herald the onset of autumn.

Autumn is a gorgeous time of year in Japan as the intense heat of summer makes way for cool breezes, bringing exquisite red and yellow leaves. During this period, it is common for people to hike and admire the changing foliage, taking along bento boxes filled with seasonal foods.

Some of the nation's most delicious food becomes available in the autumn. It is the best time to savour the freshness of Japan's rice, as restaurants will often proudly announce they have *shinmai* (new harvest) rice. Produce such as persimmons, chestnuts, pears, figs, pumpkin and sweet potatoes are bountiful. Luxurious *matsutake* (mushrooms) are also a delicacy in autumn, typically enjoyed for their rich, nutty aroma. Foods from the ocean include Pacific saury, salmon, salmon roe and octopus. Festival-goers can enjoy rice cakes at moon-viewing events, owing to the belief that the surface of the moon looks like rabbits pounding rice cakes.

Winter can be incredibly cold in Japan, particularly in the northern Tohoku and Hokkaido regions, where many prefectures are blanketed under snow for months on end. This begets a lot of hearty home cooking focused on warming foods. Many people enjoy hotpots, stews and soups, with an 'anything goes' menagerie of ingredients tossed in. *Oden* is a hotpot dish associated with winter; it's composed of *daikon* (radish), fish cakes, eggs, seaweed and rice cakes in a broth. Winter vegetables are often roots, such as *daikon* and lotus root. Winter seafood is incredibly delicious, particularly yellowtail, tuna and oysters.

A winter oyster hotpot at the Michelin-starred restaurant Chimatsushima, Miyagi prefecture.

Winter

Rice

Rice has been the most important element in the Japanese diet since its introduction, and is one of the primary signifiers of Japanese culture. It is impossible to examine the aesthetics of the nation's cuisine without considering rice, its staple food, the star of the traditional meal. According to food scholar Naomichi Ishige, former Director-General at the National Museum of Ethnology in Osaka and current Professor Emeritus, 'Traditional Japanese cuisine was developed with the goal of [honing] skills to match the taste of rice cooked without any seasoning, and of sake made from rice.'

The classic Japanese meal, or *Ichiju Sansai*, has rice as its main element; a primary dish, two side dishes, soup and pickles are seen as condiments that complement it. Rice itself is sacred, and sake and *mochi* (sticky rice) are the most holy offerings people can make at shrines. Sake barrels are a ubiquitous sight at large shrines, as breweries ask for a good harvest.

Rice paddies are a common sight across the Japanese countryside.

The Takagi shrine at Hikifune, Tokyo, is covered in rice ball effigies. This is a play on words, as people who come to the shrine are looking for love. In Japanese, the words for 'coupling' and 'rice balls' are both pronounced *musubi*.

Sake barrels on display at Meiji Jingu Shrine in Tokyo. Rice has spiritual connotations within the Shinto faith.

Although the popularity of Western foods, such as bread and pasta, have led to a decrease in rice consumption, it is still the star of any Japanese meal.

Rice is one of the most important aspects of symbolism within Japanese faith and folklore. It is a motif commonly seen in rituals, art and religion, and is an intrinsic part of the country's identity. Rice was also historically used as currency in lieu of money, even to pay taxes. It is said there are 88 gods residing in a grain of rice, as the *kanji* (written characters) for the word 'rice' are made up of the characters for '88'.

The national religion of Shinto is animistic, celebrating multitudes of gods who are seen to inhabit inanimate objects such as rocks and even the wind. The most important rice-related Shinto god is Inari, who oversees agriculture and prevails during rice planting; Inari is said to go back to the otherworld once the harvest has finished. There are over 30,000 Inari shrines across Japan, which are often visual splendours covered with fox motifs (Inari's principal messenger). The fox is said to love Inari sushi, which is made of deep-fried tofu stuffed with rice. This dish is often on the menu at restaurants next to shrines. In addition, a large number of Shinto festivals (see page 34) are related to rice harvesting.

Rice is also prevalent in creation myths. The sun goddess Amaterasu Omikami is said to have invented rice agriculture when she helped Jimmu, the first emperor of Japan, to produce it. Jimmu was connected with agriculture thereafter, overseeing harvests and praying to the gods for bountiful crops. Japan's current monarchy is still seen as descending from Jimmu and, as such, even the reigning emperor, Naruhito, has a rice paddy on the Imperial Palace grounds, which is used in harvest rituals. Many customary days of significance are also rice-related, starting from when a baby is born.

Not only is rice ubiquitous in Japanese culture, but so is *wara* (rice straw), which can be used once the grain is removed. *Wara* is versatile and used for architecture, clothing, *mino* (raincoats), shoes, *waraji* (straw sandals) and even hugely popular cat baskets. Straw is mostly used for spiritual purposes connected with Shintoism, such as *shimenawa* and *shimekazari*, which are decorative talismans that are usually displayed around New Year's.

Yuji Sakai, a straw artisan based in Nagano prefecture, says that *wara* is believed to call in the gods, who are said to live inside it. The perimeters of *sumo* wrestling rings are also made of straw, and are perceived to be sacred spaces where anyone who enters becomes purified.

Inari Okami is the Japanese god of agriculture, rice and sake. Inari's messenger is the fox, thus shrines are often covered in fox effigies.

Wara (rice straw) has talismanic value and is often placed at shrines in the form of protective amulets, used to beckon the gods.

Festivals

At the Kasedori Festival in Yamagata prefecture, locals dance around a fire while wearing straw costumes. These are designed to resemble a legendary bird who saved the region from fire by bringing water to put it out.

Japan is a country where animistic traditions are kept alive. Shinto, its national religion, holds the belief that there are 8 million gods – a spirit in everything, from rocks to trees. For this reason, even inanimate objects are seen as worthy of reverence. Shinto *matsuri* (festivals) are organized to give thanks to the gods for the gifts that nature bestows. While estimates vary, it is thought that there are between 100,000 and 300,000 festivals annually. They often have an ethereal atmosphere, and for many locals, these celebrations are the highlight of the year.

Many of Japan's rituals are rice-related, to ask or show gratitude for a good harvest and to pray for protection against natural disasters (of which the nation has many). Festivals are elaborate prayers to the harvest gods, to ensure there is abundant food for the coming year.

TOHOKU FOOD FESTIVALS

The region of Tohoku in northern Japan is predominantly rural, with many people working in agriculture. Top-tier Japanese rice brands, like Yamagata's Tsuyahime, Miyagi's Hitomebore and Akita's Komachi, are grown in the area, and regional produce such as luxurious fruit is a strong part of the Tohoku identity. People are close to the land, which means that many of these festivals take on a much richer, more authentic atmosphere than festivals held in urban areas. As such, there are countless festivals dedicated to rice harvests, protection from natural disasters and prayers for a good catch.

The Akita Kanto features 280 poles from which 10,000 lanterns are hung.

AKITA KANTO

The Akita Kanto summer festival takes place during the first week of August, and focuses on a ritual by which one can cleanse oneself of malevolent spirits and disease. It involves hanging paper lanterns shaped like *komedawara* (bags used to store rice) from bamboo poles; they resemble rice plants before harvest.

The Japanese government's Agency for Cultural Affairs designated the festival an Important Intangible Folk Cultural Property. It has a history that dates back almost 300 years.

A Shinto priest gives blessings at the beginning of the Amekko-Ichi.

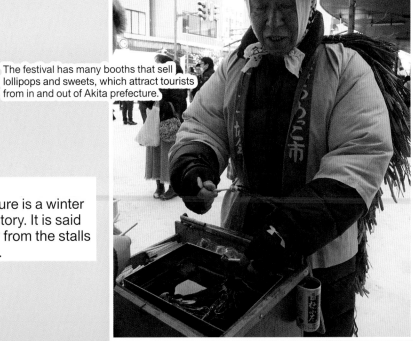

The festival has many booths that sell lollipops and sweets, which attract tourists from in and out of Akita prefecture.

AMEKKO-ICHI

The Amekko-Ichi in Akita prefecture is a winter festival with over 400 years of history. It is said that festivalgoers who buy candy from the stalls here will be protected from colds.

The Paper Balloon Festival is a way to pray for a bumper crop.

The balloons, which are made of paper, are sent into the night sky during the time of the heaviest snow in Tohoku.

KAMIHINOKINAI PAPER BALLOON FESTIVAL
The Paper Balloon Festival at Kamihinokinai in Akita prefecture is a winter event where 100 enormous paper balloons are painted with motifs like women and samurais and released into the sky. The event brings luck for good harvests and health throughout the year.

Both the horses and humans attending the Chagu Chagu Umakko wear colourful outfits.

Horses are an important part of the family for farmers in Iwate. 'Chagu Chagu Umakko' is an onomatopoeic term that describes the bells that hang off the horses.

CHAGU CHAGU UMAKKO
Chagu Chagu Umakko in Iwate prefecture takes place in June and is a sight to behold, as over 100 horses are lavishly embellished and paraded from Takizawa to Morioka cities after being blessed at the local shrine. Horses are an important part of agriculture in Iwate, and were historically seen as part of the family. Traditional homes here are L-shaped, and horses once lived inside with people.

The Enburi Festival is believed to have started during the Kamakura period (1185–1333) and is famed for its beautiful folk dances.

There are two types of dances: the *Naga-enburi*, which is slow and elegant, and the *Dosai-enburi*, which is more elaborate.

Children dressed as Ebisu, the god of fishing.

ENBURI

The Enburi Festival in Aomori prefecture, which is focused on a dance ritual to pray for a good harvest, takes place in winter. The dance takes its name from an agricultural tool called the *eburi*, and is performed to wake the gods of the rice fields and to spiritually imbue the soil with the energy of the people. The dancers wear hats in the likeness of horse's heads, and the movements resemble those of rice cultivation.

Locals at the Iizaka Fighting Festival.

Several floats crash into each other in a mock fight.

IIZAKA FIGHTING FESTIVAL
The Iizaka Fighting Festival takes place in October in Iizaka, Fukushima prefecture. Its central event is a ritual performed to appreciate a rich harvest, featuring massive floats which crash into each other in a mock fight.

Kasedori is one of the most comical-looking traditional festivals.

A shopkeeper throws water onto a Kasedori dancer, even though it is in the middle of winter.

KASEDORI

Tho Kacodori Fcstival in Yamagata prefecture is an homage to a legendary bird who brought water in order to protect villagers from fires. It is a comical spectacle where locals dress in rice straw outfits and hop around like birds. The festival is a prayer for good harvests, fire prevention and a year of luck.

ダッリノ
ダッッ00

One of the delights of visiting a traditional festival is the row of *yatai* stalls serving foods that often only appear at these events.

A *yatai* that specializes in chilli.

A girl at a Japanese festival enjoying typical food purchased at a *yatai*.

Taiyaki, a type of sweet cake that is baked in a metal mould, is a staple at summer festivals.

YATAI

Yatai are food carts that have been around since the fifth century, and were traditionally situated outside places of worship for pilgrims. The contemporary version flourished in the Edo era, serving what was then Japanese-style fast food (such as soba noodles) so commoners could get meals on the go. They also served men who were away from their families and had been ordered by their feudal lords to spend time working in the capital.

There are regional differences in the form a *yatai* can take, but in the early days, the most common type was man-powered, like a cart, moved by a balance bar. Another kind, which didn't move at all, served sushi and tempura – hence it is possible to say that *yatai* food is the genesis of Japan's most famous representative cuisine. Over time, *yatai* also helped spur many regional food booms, such as Hiroshima *okonomiyaki*, and popularized snacks that are usually only seen at festivals, such as chocolate-covered bananas and candied apples.

When the end of the Sino-Japanese War (1937–45) brought a drop in military demand for iron, foundries switched to the civilian market, making products for baking. They offered a variety of bakeware at reasonable prices that even street stall merchants could afford, such as equipment to make *taiyaki* and *ningyoyaki* (cake-like sweets). These had been created one after another in the late 1800s.

During the US occupation after World War II, food rationing meant that all outdoor stalls were banned. They were replaced by illegal markets, which were predominantly present in large cities and sold a wide range of items, from food to daily necessities. Rice was scarce, but the US eventually provided the nation with wheat, which saw the rice of *yatai* foods like *okonomiyaki* (pancake-style fritters), yakisoba and *takoyaki*, which are some of the most ubiquitous *yatai* items today. As these operations weren't legal, there were several million arrests of *yatai* owners from 1946 to 1950. They still have a reputation for being connected to the *yakuza* and have often been operated by immigrants from nations that were colonized by Japan.

Yatai have slowly become an endangered species, restricted by the Japanese government due to hygiene regulations such as the Food Sanitation Act (1947), the Fire Service Law (1948) and the Road Traffic Act (1952 and 1960). The 1964 Olympics in Tokyo were seen as an opportunity to eliminate what were deemed unhygienic food-preparation practices from the city. However, some regional *yatai* in places like Fukuoka resisted by organizing unions, and *yatai* owners persevered politically.

Nowadays, *yatai* are often only visible during *matsuri* (festivals; it is said that the reason why there are so many food stalls at festivals is because the gods like to visit jubilant places). They are run by young entrepreneurs in the same vein as food trucks abroad, selling all manner of cosmopolitan cuisine. The best place to see old-school *yatai* carts is in Fukuoka, which still boasts over a thousand of these intimate eateries.

Okonomiyaki is one of the famed *yatai* foods.

Wagashi

Wagashi are artfully prepared traditional Japanese sweets. Coming in shapes that are more akin to mini sculptures than food and with delicate colour usage, the variety of delicacies that fall under the *wagashi* banner are countless. They are typically consumed with green tea and are made with a wide range of ingredients, such as chestnuts, boiled azuki bean paste, rice, rice flour and sesame paste, with the key elements being soy beans, grains, fruit and sweetener.

The aesthetics of *wagashi* are dictated by the four seasons and the associated emotions and feelings that come with each time period. The old Japanese calendar is made up of days of significance – for example, the autumn equinox and the winter solstice. Within the seasons, Japanese culture celebrates specific moments, like the falling of cherry leaves and the first frost. These evoke a visual poetry, and it is these concepts that *wagashi* try to recreate.

Chrysanthemum-themed *nerikiri wagashi* from Yamamoto-tei in East Tokyo.

Motifs change entirely from month to month. For example, in January, they are typically pine, bamboo, cranes and turtles. In February, there are many Japanese apricots and peach blossoms. Summer sweets are typically jelly-like, suggesting dewy images of monsoons, with decorations like hydrangeas and mandarins. *Mizu yokan*, a type of watery red bean sweet, is wrapped in bamboo to make it appear cooling. Autumn sweets use chestnuts and chrysanthemum motifs. However, nothing evokes more bountiful visual references than the cherry blossoms of spring. At that time, all the sweets take on sublime pastel hues with billowing pink gradations.

Hanami dango (rice flour dumplings) bought at a grocery store and eaten at Asao River during cherry blossom season.

Takeshi Tone, owner of the Tone confectionary shop in Mie prefecture, explains, '*Wagashi* is really fascinating in that it doesn't use that many ingredients, but we can produce tens of thousands of sweets. It can take seven years just to learn the technique. To make delicious sweets there are three important things: you need to use the best ingredients; next is the recipe; then the technique. These elements together in harmony are the beginning of making delicious sweets. But these aren't enough by themselves to satisfy customers: you also need to engage their feelings.'

The history of *wagashi* spans over 2,000 years, starting with nuts ground into a powder and *mochi* rice cakes. Developing alongside the Japanese tea ceremony and influenced by Western sweets, *wagashi* have evolved substantially over the years. The late Edo period was a time of peace which saw the quality rise significantly, as ingredients became more available to the masses. The Meiji period, an era characterized by rampant Westernization, saw the importation of culture from abroad, as well as the adoption of Western technology such as the oven. As such, *wagashi* are an ever-evolving concept, as their makers constantly try out new ingredients and techniques.

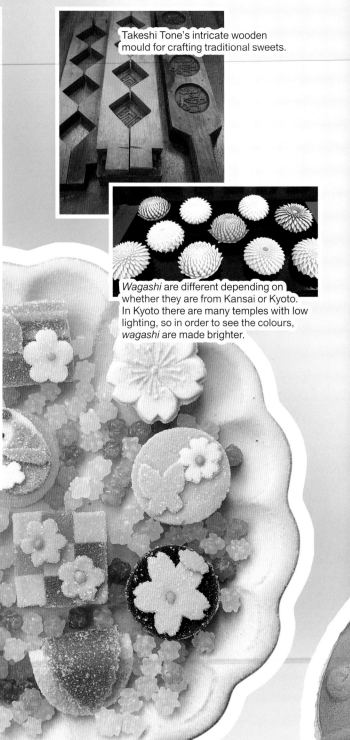

Takeshi Tone's intricate wooden mould for crafting traditional sweets.

Wagashi are different depending on whether they are from Kansai or Kyoto. In Kyoto there are many temples with low lighting, so in order to see the colours, *wagashi* are made brighter.

Kawaii and kitsch spring-themed sweets.

Rose *nerikiri wagashi* from Gora Hana Kotoba in Kanagawa prefecture.

Goldfish *yokan wagashi*, a staple during summer.

Leaf-shaped *nerikiri wagashi*.

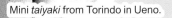

Mini *taiyaki* from Torindo in Ueno.

Sakura-themed *yokan wagashi* from tea room Mube in Tokyo.

Gift-Giving

The giving of gifts is an intrinsic part of Japanese culture. *Omiyage* are souvenirs that are brought back from trips (both domestic and international), and *temiyage* are gifts you take when you visit someone. Gift-giving is seen as a polite gesture and a means of communicating gratitude, but is also obligatory in some cases. At its core, it's a symbolic way to suggest a relationship is close and meaningful and to express gratitude. Items are often ornately wrapped, and the revealing of layers is one of the surprises of receiving a gift. While there are no rules as to what should be given, gifts in sets of four are avoided, as the word for 'four' is phonetically the same as that for 'death'.

Musk melons are incredibly expensive, and usually only seen in the context of gifts.

パク
パク

In the domain of gift-giving, fruit maintains a luxurious position.

The quality of Aomori apples is maintained due to farmers' cultivation methods (they use up to 10 techniques before harvesting).

Peaches are a luxury fruit grown in Okayama and Fukushima prefectures; they're a common gift.

Omiyage are a huge industry, and presents from domestic locations are often food-related. Localities will exploit their famed regional delicacies to full effect, offering limited-edition items that are only available in certain places. For example, Akita is renowned for its *kiritanpo* (rice that is pounded and shaped into long sticks) and Fukushima is known for peaches, so entire shelves will be lined with peach-themed gifts. Aomori boasts some of Japan's most delicious apples, and visitors can stock up on apple jams, drinks and products like Sweet Aomori Apple Pie KitKats. Often, the packaging is more elaborate than the product within. Not only is the food itself a gift, but many local souvenirs take on the guise of famed produce and foods, such as folk toys in the likeness of Kitakata ramen.

Another gift-related custom is that of *ochugen* and *oseibo.* Although increasingly less common – particularly among young people – these are twice-yearly affairs in summer and at year end (when workers receive bonuses) when colleagues and relatives give gifts that are often food-related. High-end department stores will offer elaborate boxes to be given as gifts, and the packaging is of paramount importance.

While these customs are becoming increasingly obsolete, other Western-derived occasions, such as Valentine's Day and Christmas, are now massive gift-giving days. In the 1950s, Japanese sweets companies started to manufacture heart-shaped chocolates for Valentine's. In Japan, females give gifts to males on 14 February; this is thought to be due to an initial translation error made by a chocolate company executive. The custom is so widespread now that no one thinks anything of it. Quite often these are obligatory, rather than representing a real love interest. Women receive gifts the following month on White Day, 14 March. Birthdays are also an occasion for giving food gifts, meaning there is a year-round demand for edible presents.

One extremely common gift in Japan is fruit, which is seen as a way to enjoy seasonality (for example, the perfection of early summer Yamagata cherries). Fruit is also perishable, so won't take up room in people's homes. Historically, it is used for religious offerings in Japanese culture, as people often have a Buddhist altar on which they will place fruit or rice. During the Meiji era, more exotic fruits were imported from Europe and the US, giving many of these items a cachet that has remained ever since.

An industry revolving around luxury fruit surfaced during the bubble era after World War II, bringing with it incredibly time-consuming and labour-intensive farming processes, such as pollinating blossoms with a brush by hand, placing 'hats' on fruit so it doesn't burn, and creating odd shapes, like square watermelons. Luxury fruit shops that sell astronomically-priced musk melons and cultivated fruit like *Hatsukoi no Kaori* (white strawberries) have popped up in exclusive shopping districts, such as Tokyo's Ginza. Invariably, they are placed in exquisite cases, such as wooden paulownia boxes, and presented like jewellery.

Cherries grown in Yamagata are a luxury fruit of unparalleled perfection. They look like jewellery rather than food.

Bento Boxes

Mascots

THEME PARKS

Kawaii Food

Café Culture

SHINY APPLE JUICE

Branding

果汁100%

Contemporary Cuisine

Bento Boxes

Bento are single-portion portable meals usually arranged in boxes. The ones seen here were all made by *chara ben* artist Momo.

A bento box is said to be a form of charming communication between the maker and the person it is made for.

Five billion bento boxes (visually pleasing packed meals) are made every year in Japanese homes. They are compartmentalized into sections, and usually filled with rice as a staple, then garnished with a colourful array of vegetables, meat, fish and other side dishes. Sometimes they contain salad, a fried piece of seafood, meatballs or even fruit. Each item is presented separately so that the flavours don't mix together. Opening the lid of a bento box often brings with it an element of surprise and joy at the visual arrangement within. They are eaten by children at school, but an overwhelming number are prepared for adults who take them to work or on hiking trips.

'Bento' first appeared as a term during the Edo period. Initially, they were eaten at *kabuki* theatres (a practice still popular today) and at picnics, such as those for cherry-blossom viewing. Nowadays, they are seen as a healthier option to takeaway food and an easy way to eat more vegetables. Parents prep gorgeous ensembles for their children before they leave for school in the morning, and social media has turned this activity into an ever-extravagant showcase of creative cooking prowess.

Chara ben is a craze that started in the 2000s in which over-the-top bento boxes are made in garish colours, often using popular characters such as Pikachu from the Pokemon franchise and Sanrio's Hello Kitty. These incredibly creative affairs have become a social media trend; the hashtag for *chara ben* in Japanese has millions of posts.

Momo is a popular *chara ben* artist with over half a million followers on TikTok who excels at making three-dimensional characters with rice by utilizing the hues of her ingredients. She thinks that the visual appeal of her food is an extension of traditional foods such as *nerikiri* (Japanese confectionary). As with most *chara ben* artists, the large majority of her output includes references to, or parodies of, existing characters, as well as seasonal motifs.

Classic bento usually have rice as the staple, with pickles and side dishes – however, they have taken on increasingly extravagant iterations.

Originally, bento were made by mothers for their children, but lately people have started to make them for fun, even for themselves.

It is now popular to create bento in the likeness of original characters, or popular anime or manga protagonists.

Mascots

Yuru-chara are local mascots whose purpose is to promote regional products and landmarks. The term '*yuru-chara*' was coined in 2004 by illustrator Jun Miura. It's an amalgamation of the words *yurui* (loose) and *kyara* (character), and connotes that mascots are light-hearted and comedic. They are frequently quite odd; many of them feature ridiculous themes and designs. And, despite representing specific prefectures, they retain a somewhat subversive appeal. According to Miura, *yuru-chara* mascots should represent a love of their local region and should be unique, with unsophisticated behaviour.

Mascots gather at the Furusato Matsuri at Tokyo Dome, a festival that celebrates local foods.

Sanomaru, the official mascot of Sano City, has a noodle bowl head and a potato sword.

SANOMARU

Kibichi is a mascot for Odori Park in Sapporo, where corn is sold from carts.

Yahata Inu

Kibich

Yahata Inu is the mascot of Kai City, and is a cross between a potato and a dog.

Melon Kuma is a mascot from Yubari City in Hokkaido. Recently, bears have been ravaging the area's melon fields before harvest. In reference to this, Melon Kuma has eaten so many melons that its appearance has mutated.

MOKAPYON

Melon Kuma

Mokapyon is the mascot of Moka City. It wears strawberry pants, and there is a train on its head.

The *Yuru-Chara* Grand Prix, which began in 2010, enables people to proactively participate in fandom by voting for their favourite characters. The most popular, such as Funassyi and Kumamon, see fans lined up for hours just to watch them dance in an extremely amateur manner. Fans can also have pictures taken with their favourite characters. Pre-Covid sales of goods related to Kumamon, the black bear mascot of Kumamoto, reached 157.9 billion yen (£93 million) in 2019.

While mascots can represent landmarks and famous historical figures, they are overwhelmingly food-themed, with the region's *meibutsu* (specialities; see page 85) incorporated into their designs. Quite often, a character itself is made of a local agricultural product, such as fruit.

Nyango Star has performed in Saudi Arabia, Spain, Chile and Sri Lanka.

NYANGO STAR

Nyango Star is the *yuru-chara* for Kuroishi, a remote region in Aomori known for its outstanding apples. Besides promoting local products, Nyango Star is a heavy metal drummer and plays covers of famous songs at unlikely locations, such as children's theme parks and shopping malls. It has become a viral sensation, with some of its most popular YouTube videos garnering over 10 million views. Its videos have even been tweeted by musicians such as Queen's Brian May and the late Joey Jordison from Slipknot. Nyango Star also has its own band with other popular mascots, Charamel, and has released original tracks.

Most mascots are created by an area's prefectural government, and the designs are usually the result of nationwide competitions. However, Nyango Star is rare in that it is made by an individual creator who also plays it during live appearances. Its actual identity is a secret.

Nyango Star, *yuru-chara*

How did Nyango Star come about?
[NS]   I thought of it myself. I am Kuroishi born and bred. Aomori is an apple production area, my home is an apple farm and I had a cat, and that became the inspiration. I can illustrate as well, so I also made the design. I thought, I can do the whole thing myself. I think that is rare.

What kind of place is Kuroishi?
[NS]   There is a lot of nature and festivals in summer. There is no connection between metal and Kuroishi, though. It is a place where you can relax. I personally like metal – the first time I listened to any Western music was my brother's Metallica CD. I was also into the band X Japan, which is slash metal.

Was Nyango Star popular from the start?
[NS]   No, not at all. I was just one of the many mascots out there. There is a Grand Prix which ranks the popularity of characters, and I was really at the bottom. I was drumming at a lot of events and there was one that was close to a train station. A tourist took a video and tweeted it. That went viral. I was playing X Japan's song 'Kurenai', and then Yoshiki from X Japan called me to do a show with him, and then I went on TV. After that, a video where I play the theme song to *Anpanman* [a children's TV show] went viral as well, and I had a documentary on *VICE* because of that. I was really surprised. I thought of the Nyango Star concept in 2014 and made it in 2015, but it took two years to go viral.

What is the main impact Nyango Star has had?
[NS]   Rather than selling items, I think it's made people aware of Kuroishi as a place. Nyango Star has raised its recognition level, as a lot of people don't know about other prefectures in Japan.

Nyango Star on stage at Tokyo Dome.
It admits it can hardly see out of its suit.

Bear-shaped cakes from MARINE HOUSE in Shibuya, Tokyo.

Kawaii Food

Coffee Popula in Gunma prefecture serves bear-themed parfaits and puddings.

Bear-shaped food at Kumachan Onsen in Tokyo. The bear is frozen and will melt when hot liquid is added.

Dog marzipan sweet from J COOK in Shibuya, Tokyo.

Studio Ghibli-themed sweets from Shiro-Hige's Cream Puff Factory in Tokyo.

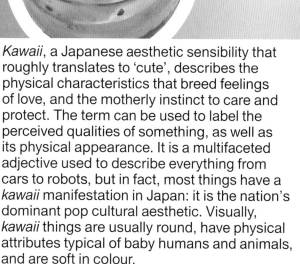

Sundae from the now-closed Kawaii Monster Café in Harajuku, Tokyo.

Kawaii, a Japanese aesthetic sensibility that roughly translates to 'cute', describes the physical characteristics that breed feelings of love, and the motherly instinct to care and protect. The term can be used to label the perceived qualities of something, as well as its physical appearance. It is a multifaceted adjective used to describe everything from cars to robots, but in fact, most things have a *kawaii* manifestation in Japan: it is the nation's dominant pop cultural aesthetic. Visually, *kawaii* things are usually round, have physical attributes typical of baby humans and animals, and are soft in colour.

    Kawaii culture has a huge presence within the world of Japanese cuisine, too. A description of 'cute' food can be found in *The Pillow Book*, written around 1,000 years ago. Adorable edible items are found in countless manifestations in Japan, from panda-shaped bread and bear-shaped hot pots to cute cafés with themed food creations. No doubt social media has fuelled the desire for food to be saccharine, colourful and pastel-coloured. While cuteness is found in savoury food, it comes as no surprise that *kawaii* aesthetics are overwhelmingly present in Japanese sweets.

A monstrous classic parfait from Cafe Tsuzuki in Nagoya, which was established in 1945.

OKINAWAN ICE CREAM

エグ
エグ

Kawaii parfaits from the Snow Brand Parlor Sapporo Flagship Shop in Hokkaido.

Blue Seal started as a milk distributor for the US military stationed in Okinawa. In 1963, they left the base and started an ice cream company.

Parfait from Aomori A-Factory, a modern complex selling local food from the region. Aomori is famous for its apples.

Cherry parfait from luxury Tokyo fruit shop Sembikiya.

PARFAITS

Parfaits are a long-lasting food fad in Japan with no end in sight. They're based on the American style of parfaits and use elements such as ice cream, whipped cream and cake, but often include Japanese ingredients like *shiratama dango* (mochi rice flour balls), red bean paste and *kinako* (soybean flour). They are then garnished with a variety of ingredients that are usually seasonal, including marron chestnuts in autumn and strawberries in winter. Regions outside of Tokyo will often flaunt their local produce atop parfaits, such as matcha green tea in Uji and cherries in Yamagata.

In large metropolitan areas, parfaits are commonly sold in cafés and fruit parlours, particularly those that sell luxury produce like musk melons and mangoes, as a way for customers to try fruit. People on the northern island of Hokkaido, which is known for superior dairy, eat ice cream even when they're experiencing sub-zero temperatures (which is roughly half the year). While it's common to finish the night with a bowl of ramen noodles, a craze for late-night parfaits started around 2015 in the nightlife area of Susukino, aided primarily by their Instagram-worthy visual quality. More than 20 shops that specialize in parfaits sprang up there, and this night-time love of parfaits has also spread to Tokyo.

AFTERNOON TEA

Like all of Japan's food, afternoon tea often reflects the seasons. One of the most famous places to enjoy this decadent spread is at The Lounge at Aman Hotel Tokyo. Their tea sets have visually extravagant themes such as Halloween, 'Strawberry Delight' and a peach-themed summer set.

Afternoon tea at The Lounge at Aman Hotel Tokyo is themed seasonally. Their Halloween set is particularly delightful.

モグモグ

Harajuku-based model and artist Kurebayashi with an enormous candy floss (cotton candy) from Totti Candy Factory.

Lightbulb drinks are also popular in Harajuku.

HARAJUKU

Harajuku is the famed capital of Japanese street style. It's the neighbourhood which gave rise to legendary street fashion magazine *FRUITS*, as well as numerous subcultures like decora and Lolita. While it has largely become gentrified, with major labels moving in and making it difficult for independent stores to survive, it is still the centre of *kawaii* fashion in Japan. It also remains the best place to see outfits of the day paraded around by purveyors of experimental style.

Besides clothing boutiques, Takeshita Street – the main road in the centre of Harajuku – boasts a concentration of street food shops serving invariably sugar-loaded, shockingly coloured Western snacks. The most famous of these are crepe stores, but there are numerous confectionary, fruit, cotton candy (candy floss), ice cream and cake shops. The street serves as a launching pad for many local or imported snack trends, such as rainbow toast from Korea.

Staple items at retro *kissaten* include puddings.

Café Culture

Spaghetti made with tomato ketchup (as opposed to paste) is a popular retro café staple.

Though you might be forgiven for thinking that Japan is a nation filled with tea houses, it is also a delight for lovers of fine coffee. Much like other customs from abroad that Japan adopted, coffee culture took on unique elements and aesthetic qualities, and roasting and brewing techniques were also refined to create a localized café scene. While there are standard international chains such as Starbucks, there is a unique tradition of *kissaten*, which are dimly-lit dens that smell of coffee. Recently, stylish cafés serving espresso-based drinks have become common. In both cases, while they are places to meet friends or colleagues, they are also spaces where one can enjoy a solitary moment with a good book.

Melon pancake from Bridge in Ginza, a café established in 1958.

Furuya in Atami, a region known for retro cafés. Lately, the area has become a popular spot for people who are enamoured with the Showa-era aesthetic.

Photogenic soda floats from Cafe Zou in Kyoto.

SHOWA-ERA *KISSATEN* (CAFÉS)

From the Edo period to the Meiji era, influences from abroad entered Japan via ports, giving them a cosmopolitan atmosphere as Westerners – and, by default, their food – appeared in areas like Yokohama. From the Meiji era onwards there was a boom in cuisine such as beef-based dishes, as Japanese food gradually became Westernized. In 1877 the nation began importing coffee, and the first café (*kissaten*) opened in 1888. Eventually, cafés started to pop up in urban areas and spread across the country.

The Taisho era (1912–1926) saw a flourishing of dishes that are considered to comprise Japanese cuisine today, but which are in fact Western fusion foods, such as *kare-raisu* (curry), *korokke* (croquette) and *tonkatsu* (pork cutlet). The Showa era that followed (1926–1989) is the longest period in modern Japanese history, starting before World War II and ending during the country's post-war economic prosperity. It was a fraught, eclectic time marked by cataclysmic change as Japan went from being a war-ravaged country to the world's second-largest economy, with its branded goods, from companies like Sony, Toyota, Nintendo, Canon and so on, taking over the world. During this time, Japan was also a leading manufacturer of products like cars and electronics (rather than outsourcing, which is the current norm).

During World War II coffee imports halted, but thrived again after the war, sparking a *kissaten* boom. When Japanese people think back on the Showa era, they often imagine the aesthetic sensibilities of the 1960s and '70s – and in fact, one of the best places to see this retro kitsch look nowadays is at Showa-era *kissaten*. Japanese-Western foods, such as inauthentic spaghetti made with ketchup, melon soda, puddings and parfaits, are a staple at *kissaten*, and are symbolic of a time of optimism and decadence that brings back waves of nostalgia.

Popular Lolita fashion icon Rin Rin at Norakuro, which serves breakfast meals typical of Showa-era cafés.

NORAKURO

Established in 1969, Norakuro is an example of a retro café with an old-school interior. It's adored by many types of patrons, from the elderly clientele who live nearby to young hipsters who are discovering the low-key charm of *kissaten*. They use a siphon to percolate their coffee, a popular method at *kissaten* coffee houses due to its performative value.

The current owner, Kazutora Nara, says that the previous owner ran the café for 30 years until Nara's mother took over in 2003. It is named after a popular manga in which a dog comes back from a war where he was deployed as a soldier and opens a coffee shop. Norakuro is famed for its delightful 'morning sets', which feature thick toast, jam, eggs and coffee or tea. Nara explains, 'It is hard to make new *kissaten* like this. It would be impossible to get permission, even though there is a Showa-era retro boom at the moment. You would have to make the interior stainless steel due to regulations, rather than [having] brick walls, so it is important to preserve places like this.'

Norakuro is an excellent example of a classic Showa-era brick café.

ESPRESSO CAFÉS

Japan is now one of the largest importers of coffee in the world, bringing in approximately 450,000 tons per year. The growth in the beverage's popularity means it even outstrips green tea consumption. The country's speciality coffee culture has flourished since the end of the twentieth century, spurring a trend for high-quality espresso cafés that resemble those in most metropolitan cities.

Muumuu Coffee is one such café in Tokyo's downtown region of Kyojima. Owner Ayumu Haitani says, 'I formerly lived in Melbourne, where the coffee culture is influenced by Italian immigrants. The influence of Australian coffee culture on Japan is undeniable; there is a geographic proximity as well.'

Haitani is part of a DIY movement to retrofit old Japanese dwellings in order to breathe new life into them; Muumuu Coffee was previously a defunct grilled pork restaurant inhabited by an elderly man and his cat. Haitani sees an undeniable link between the urban layout of the Kyojima area and the intimate community that resides there.

Rin Rin at Muumuu Coffee, an example of a Showa-era structure that has been retrofitted to make a café.

Muumuu serves some of the best espresso coffee, but is also a hub for *kendama* (cup and ball game) players and attracts a sizeable international crowd.

Kiiroitori *warabimochi* with yuzu citron and brown sugar syrup.

Korilakkuma dipping noodles with duck breast.

Temari sushi, rice ball and matcha soba set meal.

Kiiroitori *anmitsu* with ice cream and yuzu citron honey. The Rilakkuma Arashiyama Sabo Café in Kyoto serves many traditional sweets, as the city is known for its classic *wagashi*.

Korilakkuma's sweet *zenzai* (a sweet soup made with azuki beans) and salted kelp.

Rilakkuma five-layer pancake, a hearty meal resembling a pagoda, filled with yuzu jam and whipped cream topping.

CHARACTER CAFÉS

After World War II, as cafés proliferated around Japan, they gradually became seen as places for entertainment rather than simply somewhere to enjoy a coffee. Nowadays, people can visit themed establishments such as maid cafés, manga cafés, cat cafés and jazz cafés.

Japan's most prominent character companies like Sanrio (the maker of Hello Kitty) started to create fantastical themed cafés using their most popular characters too. Launched in 2003 by character company San-X, Rilakkuma is a lazy, expressionless, unmotivated bear. The character resonated with young people and quickly became extremely popular. Rilakkuma cafés are some of the most ubiquitous in Japan, but the Rilakkuma Arashiyama Sabo Café in Kyoto stands out for its classic aesthetic. Housed in a traditional tea house in a historic area, it offers a variety of traditional local dishes and sweets featuring Rilakkuma.

Rilakkuma matcha parfait with three-coloured *dango* (sticky rice balls).

THEME PARKS

Ginger sits on a sofa.

There are numerous food-related theme parks across Japan, usually run by companies as a form of advertising and a place to sell branded merchandise. They are often quite zany, and surprisingly, many are devoted to savoury foods as opposed to the expected sweets or chocolate factories. Even the most niche examples, such as the *mentaiko* (cod roe) theme park, attract an incredible number of visitors. These theme parks show the relationship between food, entertainment, corporate identity and visual branding in Japan, and are popular destinations for both international and domestic tourists.

Curtain made up of ginger replicas.

IWASHITA NEW GINGER MUSEUM

The Iwashita New Ginger Museum is an eccentric cultural institution devoted to young pickled ginger dishes produced by Iwashita, a ginger company. While ginger is a common condiment in Japan, the aesthetic of the museum is comical, with the pink phallus-shaped ingredient depicted in a variety of displays ranging from a ginger shrine to a deer with giant ginger-shaped antlers, and dubious ginger effigies sitting on sofas or in beds. There are also displays featuring the Iwashita New Ginger penlight, which is flesh-coloured and lights up. Despite the visual humour of the museum, the product is delicious, and the museum café serves pink-hued drinks and small dishes made of pickled ginger.

Displays relate to the delicious pickled ginger products made by Iwashita.

Ginger in bed, reading.

Deer with ginger-shaped horns.

Mutsugoro ramen from Hokkaido.

Unagi (freshwater eel) ramen from Fukuoka.

Zomramen from Hokkaido. The noodles are blue, and are meant to replicate a brain.

SHIN-YOKOHAMA RAMEN MUSEUM

The Shin-Yokohama Ramen Museum is a museum and food court that celebrates the popular noodle dish from China. It was established in 1994 and is the first ramen attraction of its kind. The museum gives visitors an introduction to ramen culture and its history, plus has displays related to the world of instant ramen. The main food court replicates a 1958 townscape (the year that ramen was invented) featuring realistic alleyways, retro neon and historical storefronts. There are only eight selectively chosen restaurants in the entire complex from the major ramen capitals of Japan: Sapporo, Kitakata, Hakata, Kumamoto, Tokyo and Yokohama. There is also a store selling quirky and niche brands of instant ramen that are difficult to find.

The interior of the Shin-Yokohama Ramen Museum looks like a post-war cityscape.

NAMJATOWN

Namjatown is a food amusement park inside Sunshine City, a mall in Ikebukuro, west Tokyo. Everything there is cat-themed, with cat mascots, cat goods and even a cat house of horrors. The park features numerous shops that sell cake, ice cream and candy floss (cotton candy). It is also one of the best destinations to get *gyoza* dumplings in Tokyo, as it houses a number of restaurants in an atmospheric Showa era-themed hall.

Candy floss in the shape of a cat's paw.

Namjatown is a good place to try an array of *gyoza* and ice cream, including revolting flavours like oyster and shark fin.

Cats greet guests at Tokyo's feline theme park, which is located inside a shopping mall.

MENTAI PARK

Mentaiko, a type of cod fish roe, is the most popular side dish that accompanies rice in Japan. It is commonly served as a breakfast food. To make it, the roe is soaked in a spicy chilli liquid. Each *mentaiko* is carefully processed by experienced workers.

Kanefuku, the largest producer of *mentaiko*, has created six theme parks across Japan, each called Mentai Park. According to their PR officer Yuta Watanabe, 'Our company has a factory in Ibaraki and they created the museum, as we wanted people to see how difficult and meticulous a process it is to make *mentaiko*. As such, we wanted to use the theme park to create fans.'

The park is filled with an astonishing number of visitors, many of whom are small children marvelling at the cod-roe-shaped slides, bouncy castles and games. There is a wide array of *mentaiko* dishes available, such as the ubiquitous rice balls stuffed with *mentaiko* and cod roe ice cream. Given that many Japanese people prefer Western food nowadays, *mentaiko* is often mixed with butter and used as pasta sauce or spread on baguettes.

Mentaiko graphics are emblazoned on everything, including the vending machines.

Consumers can buy fresh *mentaiko* at the park.

A dubious-sounding *mentaiko* soft serve.

The design of Mentai Park borders on the surreal. Each of its displays reference the ball-shaped roe of the *mentaiko*.

KONJAC PARK

Konjac is a starchy yam which is processed with calcium hydroxide to make the popular Japanese food *konnyaku*. Usually gelatinous in texture, it picks up the flavours of whatever it is cooked with. It is often found in oden or sukiyaki hotpots, or served sliced with miso. *Konnyaku* is lauded as a health food as it is filling and has almost no calories, but is rich in fibre.

Konjac Park in Gunma is located inside the Yokoo Daily Foods konjac factory. It is a free attraction where visitors can learn about konjac and try different manifestations of it at a buffet. Over 90 per cent of konjac produced in Japan comes from Gunma prefecture.

Konjac comes in every iteration, from sweet to savoury.

The incredibly merry-looking Konjac Park.

A konjac-themed shrine.

The theme park looks like a *kawaii* wonderland.

Branding

Octopus iconography is plastered all over Osaka, as the famed food of the region is *takoyaki* (octopus balls).

Many foods adopt local themes or landmarks as a form of local branding. This is a popular form of curry in the prefecture of Shizuoka, where there are views of Mt Fuji.

Japanese cuisine – or *washoku* – is widely renowned for its quality, artistry and taste. It is even recognized by UNESCO as an Intangible Cultural Heritage. The organization provides a definition: '*Washoku* is a social practice based on a set of skills, knowledge, practice and traditions related to the production, processing, preparation and consumption of food.'

As with other aspects of Japanese culture, cuisine is just as much about branding as the products themselves, and the demystification of food marketing and etymology can be a confusing exercise. Katarzyna Cwiertka is a scholar focused on Japan's food history, both as a domain of culture and as a window into historical inquiry that extends beyond the realms of cuisine and nutrition. She researches branding and myth creation within Japanese food extensively, and explains, 'I have an impression that the Japanese reality is becoming increasingly overtaken by branding. There is a surreal lack of distinction between what is real and what is not.'

Tochigi is famous for delicious *gyoza* dumplings. This unappetizing drink is *gyoza*-flavoured.

Local foods from Akita prefecture adopt Akita dog-themed branding.

A folk toy cow branded with a local milk company logo.

Incredibly delicious Cava-brand mackerel from Iwate, a region known for its mackerel.

Katarzyna Cwiertka, Chair of Modern Japan Studies at Leiden University, the Netherlands

Why do you think the term *washoku* is problematic?
[KC]   *Washoku* is a very good example of successful branding and invention. *Washoku* as a brand name has spread across the world. But if you ask Japanese people, they would say it is UNESCO recognized, and that comes up first in Google. However, the UNESCO description is 100 per cent false. The phenomenon is real – the word emerged in the late nineteenth century as a kind of reaction against the increasing use of the word *yoshoku* (Western food) – but *washoku* was not often used, as the words *nihonryori* or *nihonshoku* were used more. In the past, there were the categories *washoku* and *yoshoku*, so things like pork cutlets were considered to be *yoshoku*. But now, curry rice and *tonkatsu* would be categorized as *washoku*.
        My biggest problem is that the word and what is associated with it has completely changed through promotion, even though the word itself has a history – which is completely erased from its identity. Now, there is a book called *Washoku no Kotowaza Jiten* (*A Dictionary of Japanese Food Proverbs*). And in it are all kinds of food that are (ostensibly) related to *kotowaza* (proverbs) that are centuries old. But they were never about *washoku*, because these foods didn't exist. In itself the phenomenon is interesting, but from a historian's perspective, it is very problematic.

Describe the concept of *meibutsu* (regional specialities), and how *meibutsu*-branded food developed.
[KC]   It is a rather old concept, and it had a broader scope [in the past] than it has today. We associate the word *meibutsu* with food, but in the past, anything could be *meibutsu* – even a person, building or object. It meant a symbol of an area. The word has been used to characterize tourist destinations since the eighteenth century, or maybe earlier, when tourism was increasingly commodified. The Japanese have a connection between a place and its food. Now, it is so extreme that the place doesn't exist if there is no food that represents it – whether it is invented or not doesn't matter. I would say 90 per cent of *meibutsu* are new inventions.
        The funny thing about it is that Japanese consumer culture is about innovation and new trends, so there has to be new packaging. It seems like it is contradictory, because on the one hand, *meibutsu* should be traditional, but there is always a need to create new *meibutsu*. There is a strong connection between *meibutsu* and *omiyage* (souvenirs).

What are examples of famous *meibutsu* that are completely invented?
[KC]   *Raicho* (ptarmigan) is a type of bird, a protected species in the Alps. *Raicho no Sato* are Western-style waffles, but there is no connection to the bird; the only bird-related thing is the name and the image on the packaging.
        What I find fascinating is that the connection between food, souvenirs and *meibutsu* is often the natural environment, not actual food. It is not the same as local specialities in France or Italy, which are foods produced in the area. The most outrageous one is Tokyo Banana. The only connection with Tokyo is the name. There are no bananas grown in Tokyo. Simply putting the name of the place in there is sufficient sometimes.

How does branding overlap with gift-giving culture in Japan?

[KC]   With gifts, the packaging is more important than what is inside in 80 per cent of cases. The whole point of *omiyage* (souvenirs) being popular is not how something tastes – often, they don't taste good at all, and very often they are produced in the same factory and packaged differently for different areas. The point is to find something that is entertaining, and increasingly, this is done with the packaging design. I found this *omiyage* from Nara which is called *shika no fun* (literally 'deer poo'). It is about the shock effect.

What makes packaging in Japan different to that found overseas?

[KC]   There is a huge variety of packaging in Japan: kitschy, minimalist and *kawaii* (which is kind of growing outside of Japan). In the 1980s, Western style became more upscale, but the more Westernized Japanese consumer culture becomes, the more the traditional designs also move up on the scale.

What is the connection between pilgrimages and Japanese food?

[KC]   Mass tourism in Japan has a connection with pilgrimages – people embarking on a trip to visit shrines and temples. Since the seventeenth century, temples have branded themselves by saying, 'We have this statue.' Mass tourists would walk slowly along their route, where there were businesses set up, often by affluent farmers, who thought, 'I can make this rice into *mochi* and sell it as rice cakes and call it "so-and-so" rice cakes, because it is near this famous place.'

Travel as a subject area in the publishing industry began in the Edo period in the late eighteenth century. The people responsible for putting together a travel guide would go around an area and ask, 'Do you have some famous food here that we can put in our book?' If there wasn't one, they would often invent it.

Aomori is famed for its apples. There is an over-the-top celebration of them in the prefecture.

Tokyo's most popular souvenir, the Tokyo Banana. However, the city has no connection with bananas whatsoever.

青森県産
りんご

A Shirakawa daruma (roly-poly doll based on the likeness of Bodhidharma, the founder of Zen Buddhism) depicted as a bowl of ramen. The region is famous for delicious ramen noodles.

Folk toys like *kokeshi* often incorporate local products in their designs. These, by Yasuko Shiratori, have cherry and safflower motifs, as they are the famous products of Yamagata.

Manga

FOOD SAMPLES

Vending Machines

Design Festa

BENTO ARCHITECTURE

Wonder Festival

Pop Culture and Design

Manga

The Kyoto International Manga Museum is a library and museum facility that has approximately 300,000 items in its inventory. It was established as a joint project between the city of Kyoto and Seika University and serves as an important hub for manga-related research, housing many rare artefacts dating back to the Edo era.

Yu Ito is an author, researcher and curator who organizes numerous exhibitions at the museum as well as at venues abroad. He views manga as an important way to disseminate information about local cuisine and food trends. As he explains, food in manga often mirrors people's social relationships (either positively or negatively). Cuisine can thematically function as a tool to dissolve adverse feeling between lovers, friends, or family. Moreover, because manga is read in everyday situations, reading it while eating is a typical way of enjoying it – meaning the relationship between food and manga goes beyond the content on the pages.

Cooking Papa is a manga about a salaryman who can cook well. Recipes for the food depicted in each chapter are provided.

Oishinbo is a manga whose main character is a cynical food critic named Yamaoka.

Yu Ito, curator and researcher

What are the positive characteristics attributed to food in manga?

[YI]　In modern Japanese society, which has been influenced by the West, imported ideas regarding health have a strong influence on the way people think about food. Put plainly, eating something because it's delicious is viewed negatively, and eating something because it is good for your body has become one of the important criteria for eating 'correctly'. An important work in the history of manga, Oishinbo, is the first manga to sublimate information on eating correctly into entertainment – but on the other hand, gluttons who ignored their health were often depicted as outlaws or mavericks. For example, the main character in Motohiro Den's Funsou Deshitara Hatta Made, which can be seen as a geopolitical food manga, is the latest iteration of such an archetype.

　Straying Warrior Kabi Nagata: Go Gourmet! is an essay manga that depicts Kabi Nagata's various struggles with her eating disorder, and comprehensively and humorously portrays her suffering. In Japan, these forms of essay manga continue to grow, and among them are quite a few titles about food. The reason is that in Japanese manga culture, the boundary between writer and reader is blurry. As a result, there is a unique situation where there are many amateur manga writers, and inevitably many write about their own experiences. It is easy to choose food as a theme, because it is relevant to everyone's daily life.

Describe post-war food manga.
[YI]   With post-war unrest, the 1950s was still an era of poverty in Japan, and many children's greatest concern was getting something to eat. Child protagonists named after food, such as *Croquette Goennosuke* (Shigeru Sugiura) or *Anmitsu Hime* (Shosuke Kurakane), were very popular.

Later, in the 1970s, the cooking manga genre appeared, with hit works such as Daisuke Terasawa's *Mister Ajikko*. According to editor Nobuhiko Saito, these titles touched on the process of cooking something, and expressed food's deliciousness. However, later on, food manga developed into cooking-competition manga, such as in *Hochonin Ajihei* (Jiro Gyu; illustrated by Biggu Jo). Saito considers Mikiya Mochizuki's *Totsugeki Ramen* and *Cake Cake Cake* (Aya Ichinoki; illustrated by Moto Hagio) to be the first examples of cooking manga.

In the bubble era, 'gourmet manga', which illustrator Biggu Jo called 'eating with your brain manga', appeared. *Oishinbo*, written by Tetsu Kariya and illustrated by Akira Hanasaki, offered real information about ingredients and cooking.

In recent years, the act of eating as a theme has been popular. I think it is not unrelated that people who experienced the Great East Japan Earthquake and Covid have begun to pay attention to the everyday lives they took for granted (and lost).

Are food and identity linked in manga?
[YI]   Food-themed manga emphasize local ingredients and traditional cooking in order to evoke the hometown spirit of the characters' identities. This came about because of the rise of the nation state and the birth of Japanese identity. Pride in one's own region and being proud of Japan are inextricably linked. In this sense, from the 2000s onwards, *washoku* [see page 85] came to the fore, together with local food (as opposed to globalized cuisine). I think this trend is strongly reflected in food manga.

Conversely, since 2010, the idea that Japan is not a single culture, but multiple intertwined cultures and identities, has appeared in various political, cultural and other settings. In the manga world, it is significant that the Ainu (indigenous Japanese) culture-themed manga *Golden Kamuy* (2014–22), by Satoru Noda, was a big hit, and in it food featured heavily as a representation of Ainu culture.

Fumi Yoshinaga's *What Did You Eat Yesterday?* features a gay couple in Tokyo and the meals they share.

Mister Ajikko is a manga published in the 1980s about a young prodigy who cooks at a local restaurant.

Is food gendered in Japan?

[YI]   The #MeToo movement has grown greatly due to sexual harassment accusations in the film industry, and the reassessment of gender from a feminist point of view has developed radically within popular entertainment works, including manga.

In food manga, works in which professional chefs are the theme have often depicted masculine worlds. This is not unrelated to the fact that cooking manga developed within *shonen* (boys') manga, which in the past mostly focused on battles. However, as the trend has shifted to 'eating everyday food' manga, it has forced us to think about the gender roles that stubbornly continue in Japanese households: the idea that women are the people who cook and men are the ones who eat.

Tochi Ueyama's *Cooking Papa* from 1985 features a male protagonist who is responsible for cooking at home, and is a rather early example of a manga which proposed new gender roles when it comes to food. But in recent works, what is really interesting is that some titles have shifted the gender framework itself. Fumi Yoshinaga's *What Did You Eat Yesterday?*, from 2007, has a gay couple at the core of the story. The sight of Kenji, who seems to be enjoying the meal prepared by Shiro, who loves cooking, makes the reader happy.

Two fantastic recent food manga that also critically confront issues to do with marriage, home life and romance as social problems intertwined with gender are *She Loves to Cook and She Loves to Eat* by Sakaomi Yuzaki, which was originally published on Twitter, and *Konya Sukiyaki Dayo* by Natsuko Taniguchi, which depicts roommates Aiko and Tomoko. Aiko is bad at housework and wants to get married, and Tomoko likes housework but does not understand love very well.

Kyo Machiko won the Grand Prize at the Japan Cartoonists Association Awards for *Ichigo Senso* in 2015. It features sweets that are engaged in warfare.

ACTION COMICS

What are some of the best-known contemporary manga that feature food?
[YI]   *Delicious in Dungeon* by Ryoko Kui is a bestseller and has won various manga awards. The fact that it is not simply a parody of a fantasy RPG, but has a solid storyline, supports this work's long-term popularity. But as a food manga, it realistically depicts non-existent food and cooking. Fictitious ingredients and dishes have appeared before, like the delicious-looking 'Hitodama Tempura' in Shigeru Mizuki's *Gegege no Kitaro*. But *Delicious in Dungeon* takes advantage of the fact that ingredients and cooking which feature in manga do not need to exist in real life. Some similarly interesting works are Taku Kuwabara's *Drifting Dragons*, in which a 'Dragon Chef' appears and could be read as a metaphor for whaling, as well as the *yokai* (supernatural being) meals that appear in Atsushi Mukoyama's *Tadashii Yokai no Tabekata.* In all these titles, the procurement of food is thoroughly depicted. As a sub-genre of food manga, hunting and fishing manga have emerged as a trend in recent years, such as Yabuta Ajima's *Kuma Uchi no Onna* and Nobuhiro Midoriyama's *Wana Girl.*

Gokudō Meshi (Criminals' Meals) is a comedy about Japanese prisoners who fantasize about the best food they've ever had in the past.

Anpanman is an incredibly popular children's manga about a hero whose head is a type of sweet bean-filled bread.

Delicious in Dungeon is a comedy manga series by Ryōko Kui. It combines the food and fantasy genres.

What manga title that features food do you recommend most?

[YI]   Takashi Yanase's *Anpanman*. Originally the main character was aimed at adults, but later it became a picture book for children (in 1973) and based on this an anime was produced (in 1988). The manga version featured the protagonist, Anpanman, a super-hero whose head is made of *anpan* (a Japanese pastry made from sweet red bean paste and bread). If someone gets hungry, he flies over to them and lets them eat his head. Rather than defeating someone, the message of this work is that saving someone is a heroic act, but in saving someone else weaker than yourself, it is important to be the 'weak hero'.

Yu Ito's Guide to Food Manga

1950s

Ninja Sarutobi Sasuke, 1953 (Shigeru Sugiura). The ninjas all have appetizing names.

1970s

Rush Ramen, 1970 (Mikiya Mochizuki). The first 'cooking manga' was by a major action manga artist, and the opening scene is a gunfight!

Cake, Cake, Cake, 1970 (Moto Hagio). The pioneer of 'cooking manga' within the girls' (*shojo*) manga category.

Hochonin Ajihei, 1973–77 (Jiro Gyu and Biggu Jo). The original dishes invented in this manga, such as black curry containing narcotics, are impressive.

1980s

Oishinbo, 1983–2014 (written by Tetsu Kariya; illustrated by Akira Hanasaki). Main character Shiro Yamaoka (a journalist) and his father compete to create the ultimate menu that captures the essence of Japanese food. The two are not cooks, but the scenes in which they show off their culinary knowledge are a highlight. Many real-life restaurants also make appearances.

Cooking Papa, 1985– (Tochi Ueyama). One of the reasons for the popularity of this series, which has continued for nearly 40 years, is that it features recipes for the dishes that appear in each story. These include original dishes such as *onigirazu* (which resembles a sushi sandwich).

Mister Ajikko, 1986–99 (Daisuke Terasawa). The main character, a junior high school student, engages in a cooking duel with a group of cooks led by Ajikko, a leading figure in the culinary world. Terasawa has since had hits with *Shota no Sushi* and other food manga.

Ajiichimonme, 1987–99 (Yoshimi Kurata and Zenta Abe; original story by Yukie Fukuda). This realistic food manga looks at the craftsmanship of a chef who works at a *ryotei* (Japanese-style restaurant).

Throughout History

1990s

Kodoku no Gurume, 1994–96 (Masayuki Kusumi; illustrated by Jiro Taniguchi). Kusumi made his debut with *Yakou*, featuring a man who eats his *ekiben* (a bento box sold to eat on a train, with cutlery included) while mumbling to himself about the order in which to put the chopsticks on his plate. Here, he teamed up with Taniguchi, who has superb drawing skills. It was a pioneering work in the 'eating-only' manga genre of more recent years.

2000s

Gokudo Meshi, 2006–12 (Shigeru Tsuchiyama and Shohei Onishi). Prisoners play a game in which they tell stories about the delicious food they have previously eaten. This is a unique food manga in which no actual food, let alone a meal, appears!

2010s

Delicious in Dungeon, 2014– (Ryoko Kui). Set in an RPG-like fantasy world, the main character and his party travel through a dungeon, cooking and eating slime, dragons and other monsters they have defeated. The dishes with non-existent 'ingredients' look delicious.

FOOD SAMPLES

In the past when artisans took a mould, they used *kanten* (a type of gelatinous seaweed). Now, they make moulds with silicon so the surfaces can be very detailed. They also used wax up until the mid-1990s, but stopped because it had the potential to melt in summer!

Items such as stationery, covers to put on light switches and other types of products are popular as well.

Fake food displays are a common sight outside restaurants in Japan.

Anyone who has visited Japan will be familiar with the oddly realistic-looking food samples displayed outside cafés and restaurants. Takizo Iwasaki was the founder of food sample company Iwasaki, and was the first to popularize this phenomenon in the 1930s. The samples are completely handmade, with artisans colouring them and a creative director overseeing the entire process. According to Iwasaki's PR manager, Takashi Nakai, it is thought that these samples were first made during the end of the Taisho era and the beginning of the Showa era by an artisan who created anatomical body models.

Iwasaki's first-ever product appeared in an Osaka department store in 1932. Nakai explains, 'At the time, Western meals were fashionable, and the concept of eating out was really common. People from the provinces might not recognize a meal from its name, and it was an era when you couldn't take photos that easily, so the samples were easy to comprehend.'

While Iwasaki sell and lease small quantities of pre-made samples to eateries, they predominantly create custom-made samples to replicate dishes to perfection. First, a member of staff goes to take photos of the meals at restaurants and a real dish is brought back to the factory, where a silicon mould of it is taken. They then insert vinyl resin and heat it in the oven until it becomes hard. After it has cooled, they colour and assemble the parts.

Nowadays, there are around 80 artisans at the Iwasaki factory. Besides these ultra-realistic meal samples, they also make hundreds of comical goods, such as stationery in the likeness of pancakes and toast.

According to Takashi Nakai, finished meals are easier to make than specific ingredients – for example bananas, vegetables and raw meat, which are particularly tricky.

Each era in Japan has its own food trends. Lately, Iwasaki's Ganso Sample have made a lot of pancakes.

These competition pieces depicting carrots relaxing in Japanese-style curry were made by a veteran artisan. It takes around four to five years to become competent at making these samples.

Design Festa

Sausage-themed goods by Dekoboko.

Harajuku company mooosh makes food-themed toys that are scented with sweet aromas.

Cute food-themed *kokeshi* by Cokets.

Founded in 1994, Design Festa is a huge two-day arts, crafts, performance and fashion event held twice a year at the Tokyo Big Sight centre. At its peak, the festival attracts in excess of 15,000 artists. It has an 'anything goes' ethos where anybody can participate, regardless of their creative genre and level of success. It also serves as a springboard for amateur and underground artists to get noticed by a large audience.

The event's atmosphere is extremely liberal, with a heavy subcultural presence, from goth photographers to graffiti artists to toy figure designers. *Kawaii* (cute) culture heavily dominates, as many fashion tribes associated with *kawaii* (such as decora, Lolita and maids) are ubiquitous. The most prominent motif in *kawaii* crafts, fashion and goods is sweets – pastel-coloured cupcakes, strawberries, ice cream, candy and other saccharine Western treats.

Handcrafted, food-themed candles made by Em Zed Eych Candles.

Shonan Food Sample make their items with techniques that are used for realistic restaurant samples.

Felt cupcake by mococo house.

Cupcakes are likely the most popular motif in *kawaii* (cute) culture.

Gyoza-themed goods.

Milk-themed goods by Gyunyu boya (literally 'milk boy').

Em Zed Eych's pastel-hued *kawaii* creations are a cross between designer toys and candles.

While maid fashion is often associated with women who work at maid cafés, the brand mi-mi celebrates genderless style.

Vending Machines

Vending machine that serves *gyoza*.

① ②

Rice vending machines offer bags of delicious rice from local growers. This one is in Kanagawa.

Heating technology means that hot beverages and soups are now ubiquitous in vending machines. This is clam soup.

Travel to any destination across Japan, and vending machines are a constant presence along highways, roads and shops, even in the most remote parts of the country. Japan has the highest number of vending machines per capita in the world, with over 4 million, or 1 for roughly every 31 people. Their ubiquity is often attributed to the nation's low crime rate, as they can exist anywhere without theft or vandalism. Some restaurants have even installed them outside their establishments so that people can buy frozen versions of their meals at any time.

Vending machines mainly serve hot and cold alcoholic and soft drinks such as juice, tea, sports drinks and coffee. They take coins and cash, as well as prepaid cards. There are in addition food vending machines that serve ice cream, *gyoza* (dumplings), ramen, pizza and curry, among other popular foods. They also often sell *meibutsu* (regional specialities). One vending machine in Okayama prefecture even sells *wagyu* beef steak, while another in Nagasaki sells frozen sashimi.

The oldest vending machine in Japan is wooden, and was originally used to sell postage stamps. It was created in 1904 by the inventor Takashichi Tawaraya. The popularity of vending machines for use by the general public rose on the advent of the cupronickel coin in 1967, which led to an explosion of coins in circulation. In 1962, Coca-Cola brought their vending machines to Japan, which led to them being a standard way to purchase soft drinks. In 1970, machines that sold hot and cold drinks were introduced at the World Expo in Osaka. The popularity of vending machines peaked around the year 2000, with 5.6 million of them across Japan. The Covid-19 pandemic and the advantages of unmanned shopping and contactless buying brought about a revival in these glowing boxes, too.

Christopher D. Salyers is a designer and the author of the book *Vending Machines: Coined Consumerism.* Here, he explains the appeal of these ubiquitous food-dispensing apparatuses.

Christopher D. Salyers, designer and author

When did you start gaining an interest in Japanese vending machines?

[CS]   When I first visited Japan in 2006, I arrived like a doe-eyed boy lost in Shibuya at night, blinded by the vast number of vending machines lining the streets. Sure, most were simple beverage dispensers, but I'd eventually come across machines selling ice cream, books, cigarettes … the possibilities seemed endless, limited only by imagination and tech. So I started to seek them out: machines for popcorn, beer, strange capsule toys, rice, frozen fish, homemade bento boxes; vintage machines scattered about Shimokitazawa or housed like artefacts in an old arcade in Odaiba. I then found people on the internet who shared a similar passion, and this eventually led to other, more elusive machines, like ones selling cosplay outfits or sex toys.

What is the appeal of the vending machine?

[CS]   I've always had an intense appreciation for tech, and Japan has been at the forefront of robotics and automation for quite some time. So I certainly have a love for how we can simplify and improve our lives through emerging technologies. And for those of us used to the 'pay, click, consume' immediacy that the internet offers, I don't think the appeal of the vending machine is that dissimilar.

There's an old aphorism that goes: 'Change is inevitable, except from a vending machine.' There's something about our inherent need to find regularities in life, if only to ease the other, more complicated aspects of our existence. In my book, *Vending Machines: Coined Consumerism*, I profile a Japanese blogger named Motomachi. Every day, for over four years, he would photograph the same vending machine across the street from his apartment. He would sometimes sketch over the photos, detailing what had been taken out, what had moved, or what was hot or cold. I think there's an appreciation and respect there that's admirable. The vending machine, like most mechanical devices, will never stay exactly the same, but it will remain consistent.

The warm glow of vending machines is a ubiquitous sight, even in rural areas.

There are vending machines for rice, cakes, ramen and fresh cream.

The importance of vending machines grew during Covid, when people didn't want to have physical contact with each other.

There is approximately 1 vending machine for every 31 people in Japan. The one on the right here serves alcohol.

RAT SUNRISE

Rat Sunrise tyre shop in Sagamihara, Kanagawa prefecture, is home to dozens of vending machines dating back to the 1970s and '80s. The machines are maintained by Tatsuhiro Saito, the shop's owner, who either fills them with food from local restaurants or with dishes made in his own kitchen. His vending machine alley is always packed with people obsessed with vintage memorabilia.

An alley of retro vending machines at Rat Sunrise in Kanagawa prefecture.

BENTO ARCHITECTURE

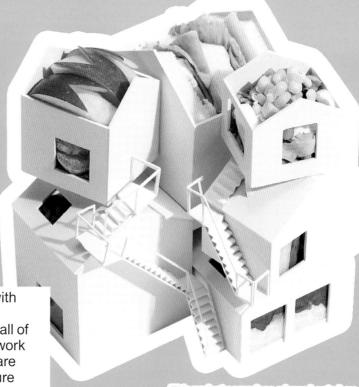

The Bento Architecture project started with four members – Takumi Sekiya, Shohei Oishi, Eimi Iida and Shunta Sakamoto – all of whom are architecture enthusiasts and work for advertising agencies. Three of them are copywriters and planners with architecture backgrounds, and the other is an art director.

During the Covid-19 pandemic, the need for advertising decreased, so when thinking about how to use their skills for other things, they dreamed up Bento Architecture. The group (which now has an additional two members, Maho Kouchi and Wataru Ito) is attracted to architecture that is structurally new and has a groundbreaking concept.

This project comprises a large bento box made up of many small bento boxes. It was inspired by Sou Fujimoto's Tokyo Apartment, a housing complex made from a series of small dwellings.

Eimi Iida, Bento Architecture design collective

Explain the concept behind Bento Architecture.
[EI]   Japan is an architectural powerhouse, a rarity in the world. However, for many people, architecture is often considered to be too complicated or difficult to be approachable.
I also feel that it is not always easy to get the meaning of architecture across to people, even when we try.
        The concept that 'good architecture makes a good lunch box' was born from the idea of making architecture more accessible, which gave birth to this project. We discovered that Japanese bento boxes are a bit like architectural models.

What do you think is the appeal of bento?
[EI]   Bento is something that everyone has picked up and is familiar with. Therefore, differences from the usual bento can be conveyed as architectural features. For example, in our Tokyo Apartment architectural bento, you will notice that the side dishes are clearly visible. This is because all the rooms in this apartment building are corner rooms with many windows.
        The 21st Century Museum of Contemporary Art in Kanazawa, which inspired one of our models, is an 'open museum', so the bento box can be turned around like a lazy susan and everyone can eat from it together.

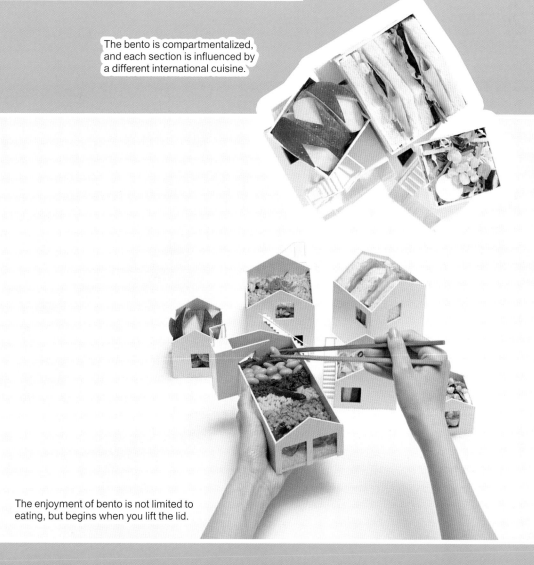

The bento is compartmentalized, and each section is influenced by a different international cuisine.

The enjoyment of bento is not limited to eating, but begins when you lift the lid.

Are there any similarities between food design and architecture?

[EI]   The way food is arranged on a plate and architecture may appear to be different concepts, but I think they are similar in that arranging food makes it look delicious, while architecture makes buildings look good. When I talk to chefs, they tell me that the architectural arrangement of food seems like a fresh idea.

In terms of Bento Architecture, the questions of how to protect the flavour in a bento and make it attractive, and how to design the architectural spaces that protect and colour our lives, are particularly similar.

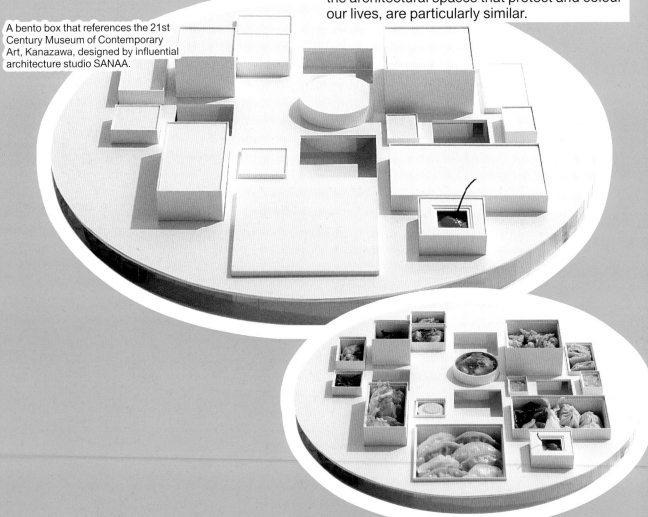

A bento box that references the 21st Century Museum of Contemporary Art, Kanazawa, designed by influential architecture studio SANAA.

The round bento box can be rotated to see a different view.

The bento consists of compartments of various shapes and sizes.

How does your collective make an architectural lunch box?

[EI]   We all bring our ideas in terms of the architecture and what kind of things would be interesting to include in the lunch. We'll come up with a number of attractive architectural ideas, but at that point we won't be sure if they overlap with the concept of how to eat. Is this a new lunch box? Does it convey the novelty of the building at a glance? How much can a single picture convey? We also take an advertising viewpoint into account when narrowing down the architecture to be used in the final output. At that time, we sometimes bring in sketches, but we also discuss cross-sections, floor plans and information on the structure of the building.

Why is the presentation of food so important in Japanese culture?

[EI]   Bento boxes, in particular, are not just a means of carrying food, but also a tool for conveying thoughts and feelings to the people who eat them. That is why the appearance of the bento box when it is opened is so important. With architectural bento boxes, we hope to use this kind of visual message to convey the architect's thoughts.

Wonder Festival

Refreshment Toy make many sweets-themed toys.

Hamburger- and omelette-themed figures.

Tempura tiger on display at Wonder Festival.

Wonder Festival is a twice-yearly convention held in Tokyo and hosted by Kaiyodo, one of Japan's largest toy manufacturing companies. The event is enormous, attracting 50,000 people with over 300 vendor booths. While the main draw is the makers of garage kits (the motifs of which are characters from anime and games), there are also numerous manufacturers of *mecha* and sci-fi character *sofubi* (soft vinyl toy) artists, as well as creators of adult-oriented figurines. The focus is on high-quality works made with meticulous detail and craftsmanship. A wide range of creations are on display, from the wares of massive toy businesses through to indie makers, who generally create items in small lots. There is also usually a large contingency of cosplayers in attendance.

A major theme in the world of Japanese toys is food, and Wonder Festival is one of the premier places to see how food is incorporated into character design. From toast to avocado to sweets to sushi, food remains a perennial staple in the iconography of figures.

Pandead are bread-themed *sofubi*.

Many booth-keepers at Wonder Festival are in cosplay or maid outfits.

Figure by designer Amamori depicting a girl holding shaved ice, a summer treat.

Wonder Festival also includes cosplayers of various descriptions. It is a liberal space with many underground-themed goods.

Wonder Festival provides indie toy creators a place to show their wares.

Designer Tomohiro Kanno's avocado-themed toys.

Pineapple monster figure by Tsutomu Miyazawa.

Vegetable-themed figure by Matsuya.

RICE FARMING

Nobuhiro Yoshida, Chef at Kozue

Bento Artistry

Buddhist Tofu Cuisine

Masayoshi 'Masa' Takayama, Masa Designs

KOPPE BREAD BAKERY

Working with Food

The tableware at Masa Designs follows the Japanese notion of *shibusa*. According to Chef Masa, embedded in this idea are the values of 'simplicity, modesty, silence, naturalness, imperfection, and normalcy.'

Masayoshi 'Masa' Takayama, Masa Designs

A sashimi ice pedestal.

Chef Masayoshi Takayama behind his world-renowned *hinoki* counter at Masa in New York City. He is one of the most celebrated Japanese chefs in the US.

Masayoshi 'Masa' Takayama is one of the world's best-known Japanese chefs. He is the owner and chef at Masa and Bar Masa, and the chef at Kappo Masa (in partnership with art gallery owner Larry Gagosian), all of which are located in New York City.

Chef Masa grew up working at his family's fish market in Tochigi prefecture, but always dreamt of moving to the US to start a small kitchen. He ended up undertaking an apprenticeship at Ginza Sushi-ko in Tokyo under the tutelage of Sugiyama Toshiaki, and eventually opened a restaurant named in its honour in Beverly Hills, California. In 2004, he opened Masa (which currently holds three Michelin stars) and Bar Masa in New York.

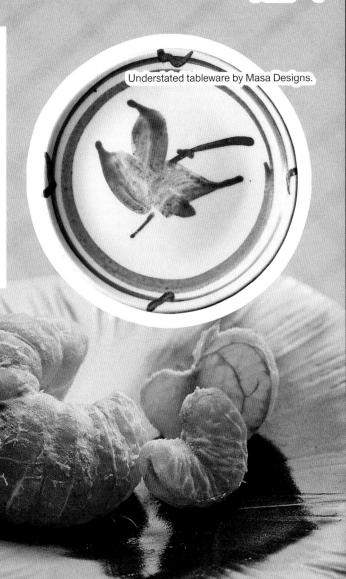

Understated tableware by Masa Designs.

A sashimi platter in earthy colours.

Chef Masa takes inspiration from nature. Here, a plate replicates a lotus leaf.

While Chef Masa's mastery of cuisine is well known, he also creates his own tableware. He is self-taught in ceramics; his interest was sparked when he was 12 and went on a class trip to a local studio at the pottery production hub of Mashiko in Tochigi prefecture. When, as an adult, he wasn't entirely satisfied with the tableware available on the regular market, he sought to collaborate with artisans to create his own understated pieces that highlight simplicity – tableware that is a supporting vessel to his cuisine.

'Food is already of value, right?' he explains. 'Food is on the plate. My ceramics design is more like using simple cloth as clothing for a person. So a main dish, sashimi, grilled fish, steamed fish; they are the main characters, right? My tableware design is like a supporting actor and character, rather than one that comes out and shows off or is very beautiful.'

Chef Masa designs the wares and provides the specifications for the pieces. He then works in collaboration with five artisans from all over Japan in remote regions such as Ibaraki, Ishikawa and Iwate, whom he has known for over 30 years.

As for the colourways, Chef Masa says, 'For food, I really prefer black. Clay, black porcelain, and black *urushi* lacquer. *Urushi* can be for a plate, bowl or a dish for seafood, and it picks up the colour beautifully. White takes away the colour sometimes, but is sometimes a good contrast with rich colours. I love *kohiki*, which is white-ish, but is a warm white, rather than white-white.'

Masa's ceramics are subdued so that the food is allowed to shine.

As Masa Designs works with artisans and all the pieces are handmade, no two are the same.

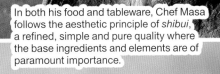

In both his food and tableware, Chef Masa follows the aesthetic principle of *shibui*, a refined, simple and pure quality where the base ingredients and elements are of paramount importance.

Shibui is a restrained elegance which favours a minimalist sensibility and is not contrived or pretentious.

Chef Masa collaborates with artisans who work with materials such as stone and wood and replicate natural forms.

RICE FARMING

Bundles of rice being dried. This is one of two traditional ways to dry rice, as there are machines (like a combine harvester) that can do it nowadays. However, the sun-drying method produces better-tasting rice.

Masato Sato's brother Katsuo making way for the reaper binder machine. He hand-cuts a section of rice to set aside temporarily. Some farmers leave a section free, without planting rice, to expedite the harvest process.

Masato Sato grows short-grain rice in Esashiku Yanagawa, Oshu, Iwate. Sato is an only child from a multigenerational rice-growing family, whose father passed away in 2022. After 36 years in the US working as a chef of French and Japanese cuisine, he decided to return to Iwate in April of the same year.

The primary method of rice cultivation in Japan is in small paddies spread over a total of nearly 2.5 million hectares (around 6.2 million acres), where seedlings are planted into the soil, rather than major-scale production like that which occurs in the US. The rice plants are well attended to, and it is extremely labour-intensive work. As many have lost the desire to farm and fewer people live in rural areas, coupled with an ageing population, the total number of paddies in Japan has lessened. Moreover, many consumers simply prefer bread as their staple food nowadays, rather than rice. During 2021 alone, the total area taken up by paddies decreased by 65,000 hectares (160,000 acres), meaning rice production will fall to below 7 million tons – the first time it has dropped that low since rice-growing data became available in 1958.

According to Sato, 'We returned to Japan to take over the family plots. My uncle is the last in our family still farming. He is 85. My cousin and I will venture into growing black rice, because it is not as commonly grown in Iwate.' These images were taken by his daughter, Aya Sato, a photographer based in the US.

Masato Sato's tractor, used for ploughing the fields in spring to prepare for planting rice.

The reaper binder machine about to be inserted into the paddy. This machine ties the ends of the bundles of rice stalks together, making them easy to dry. Masato is on the left and Katsuo on the right.

Bagged rice grains after threshing (separating grain from straw). These bags will be taken to a mill.

Bento Artistry

Soba salad referencing skulls by Edo-era Japanese painter Ito Jakuchu.

Bento that depicts 1,000-armed Kannon, the goddess of compassion. Her arms are mushrooms.

Miki Matsuura, aka Nancy, is a home chef who creates delicious-looking bento boxes (see page 54). However, rather than the *kawaii* types of bento that flood social media, she makes elaborately detailed ones that reference arthouse movies such as *A Clockwork Orange* and Wong Kar Wai masterpieces, as well as depicting musicians like David Bowie, Björk and the Sex Pistols. Nancy makes her elaborately-constructed masterpieces daily for her husband, who shares the same taste in avant-garde art. Originally a designer and illustrator, she started making bentos in 2018, which she admits were fairly normal at first, but 'gradually went in a strange direction'. She has also authored an art book featuring her creations.

A classic salmon bento that references the film *A Clockwork Orange*.

Bento inspired by Icelandic pop singer Björk.

Miki Matsuura (Nancy), bento artist

Describe your bento-making schedule.
[MM]   My husband leaves at 8 a.m., so I make them before that; he actually eats them for lunch. He gets to peep at them a bit while he is getting ready in the morning, but it's basically a surprise when he opens the lid. There are times the shape is broken by the time he opens it, but he can see what I was trying to make on Instagram!

How did you get into making *chara ben* (character bento)?
[MM]   My son really hated regular *chara ben*. He was going to a boys' school and found them embarrassing, but I really wanted to make them. He is grown up now, so I made an Instagram account, and I was wondering what to post. I was aiming to be a cool cooking Instagrammer, but I failed at that, so I decided to make bento. I couldn't make them at first, but gradually I became more technically proficient. I've never made things like Miffy or Hello Kitty.

What is appealing about *chara ben*?
[MM]   It's that it's not just for eating, but also the visuals. It is something you make for someone else usually, and it facilitates deeper and more interesting communication. I don't do motifs which are trending, like Pikachu – I just do what I like. I also play around with verbal puns, like 'Abbey Road' is 'Ebi Road' ('prawn road') and 'Mick Jagger' is a pun on '*niku jaga*' (meat and potatoes). Sometimes I will get hints from the ingredients, like the texture of curry bread seemed suitable for Donald Trump's face. I wanted to show his shamelessness, and the puffiness of the bread seemed to fit his personality.

Chewbacca made of soba noodles.

A bento that references killer Jason Voorhees' mask from the horror film *Friday the 13th*.

Why is food presentation so important?
[MM]   I think it has to do with relationships. Japanese females – especially ones our age [Nancy is in her late 50s] – tend to be overly considerate. When someone comes to your house, they are like, 'Have this! Eat this! Please take this!' There is a notion of wanting to make others joyful. It goes above and beyond empathy. When I make bento, I am thinking about whether the other person will get a kick out of it.

Besides presentation, what is important to consider when making bento?
[MM]   It is food, so I am really careful actually. For example, I will use ingredients according to whether it's hot or cold outside. When it is cold, I add warm miso soup in a soup mug. When it is hot, I have to be really careful about sterilization and hygiene. I put a cooling pack in with the bento, so I won't use ingredients that will go hard because of the ice pack. Also, I have to introduce variety so my husband doesn't get bored. I'll wonder if he might want something different and make a curry. I take balance into consideration, so I will add a salad, or another bento altogether. In summer, because people have less of an appetite in the heat and humidity, I make the bento with *somen* noodles, using cold soup.

This Noh theatre mask bento is made from potato salad.

HOW TO MAKE A BENTO BOX, WITH NANCY

'From *Ziggy Stardust* to *Blackstar*, David Bowie is the eternal star – and fittingly, this is an ephemeral bento lunch box which can be eaten quickly and then disappears.

　　This bento was made while I was in a state of deep emotion after watching the Bowie documentary *Moonage Daydream*. I used an artistic bento box made of lacquer by Eiichi Shiki, which has moon and octopus motifs.'

Mix white rice, black rice (wild rice) and edible charcoal powder and cook. Mix with sushi vinegar to make black sushi rice.

Paint on *oblaat* (a thin, edible layer of starch) using charcoal powder dissolved in water.

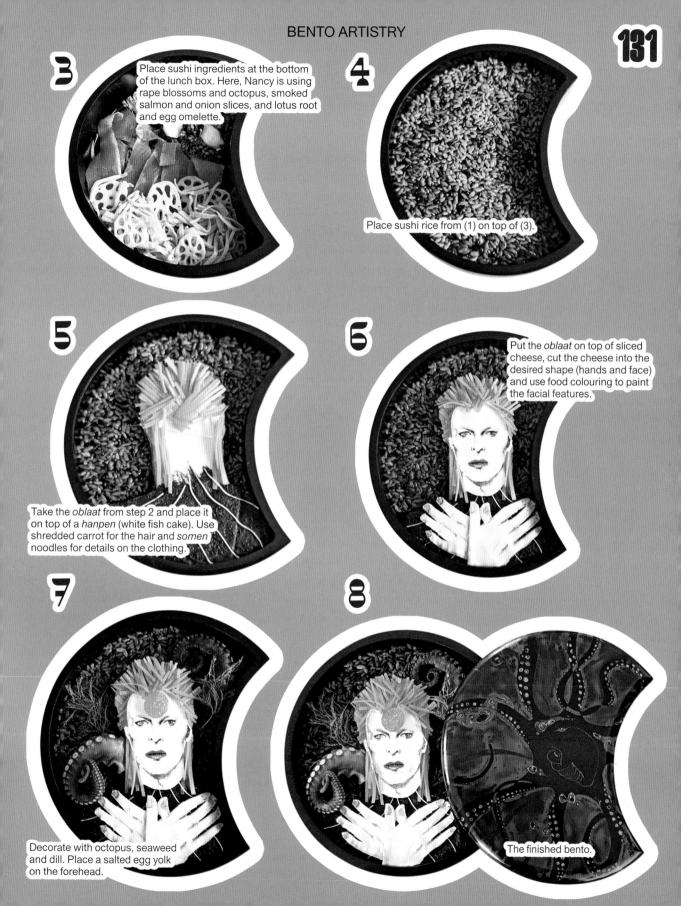

3 Place sushi ingredients at the bottom of the lunch box. Here, Nancy is using rape blossoms and octopus, smoked salmon and onion slices, and lotus root and egg omelette.

4 Place sushi rice from (1) on top of (3).

5 Take the *oblaat* from step 2 and place it on top of a *hanpen* (white fish cake). Use shredded carrot for the hair and *somen* noodles for details on the clothing.

6 Put the *oblaat* on top of sliced cheese, cut the cheese into the desired shape (hands and face) and use food colouring to paint the facial features.

7 Decorate with octopus, seaweed and dill. Place a salted egg yolk on the forehead.

8 The finished bento.

Nobuhiro Yoshida, Chef at Kozue

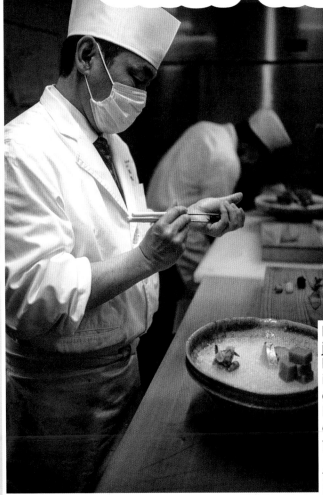

Chef Yoshida in the kitchen at Kozue, a Japanese restaurant inside the iconic Park Hyatt Hotel in Shinjuku. Its menu changes every month, as the use of seasonal ingredients is the foundational essence of *kaiseki*.

Nobuhiro Yoshida is a Tokyo-born chef who joined Kozue, a Japanese restaurant with breathtaking views on the 40th floor of the iconic Park Hyatt Hotel, in 1996, and took on the role of Chef de Cuisine in 2020. While he refined his skills at various fine dining establishments in the city, he has spent many years at Kozue.

Yoshida is known for his forward-thinking outlook on traditional *kaiseki* cuisine. His ethos encapsulates the best elements of classic Japanese cooking: a focus on seasonality and procurement of the highest-quality ingredients, along with innovative presentation, to create a spectacle for the eyes – as well as the taste buds.

Nobuhiro Yoshida, Chef, Kozue

What is the concept of Kozue?

[NY]   Most Japanese restaurants [at the time] were really doing traditional *kaiseki* style, with small, individual plates. But to match the concept of the [Park Hyatt] hotel, Kozue wanted to do cutting-edge, pioneering cuisine. All the items were arranged on one plate, according to the number of people, which allowed diners to take their own food rather than it being served to them; this instigates conversation and movement.

Kozue also did things like serving items on a bowl of ice. Thirty years ago, there was nothing like that, and it was really innovative. Park Hyatt received a lot of attention when it opened, as luxury hotels were rare. Within the restaurant industry, Kozue was focused on as well. At the time, everyone started to copy our presentation. Also, the hotel is a space with very high ceilings and a sense of openness – and because it has this architectural style, we wanted to match the food visuals to the space.

Counter-seated *kappo*-style restaurants (with the chef cooking in front of the guest) usually get Michelin stars, but we are in a hotel, so we are in the back. The guests don't see us or smell the cooking, but we have to titillate them and have them enjoy the meal dish by dish. We also have a lot of foreign guests, so we have to decide how to express Japanese food.

At a regular *kaiseki*, each serving is split up. However, at Kozue, all items are put on the dish and the diners can enjoy the presentation.

Knife skills on display whilst cutting *toro*, the fatty belly of a tuna. Yoshida says, 'There are many fish that you see in our kitchen that were swimming in the ocean yesterday.'

How important is seasonality in Japanese food?

[NY] It is the most important element. The Japanese love and celebrate the seasons, and we express that in our meals. I think spring and autumn are the most inspirational seasons for food. In spring, winter has finished and there is an abundance of ingredients. We change everything over the four seasons, at the beginning of April, July, September and December.

The food really changes and the presentation completely changes as well. Within Japanese food there are concepts like *shun* [fresh local, seasonal food]. But nowadays, there are young bamboo shoots in January and February, and other types in May and June – however, it is established knowledge that they are most delicious in March and April, so I will try and use them then.

We also express seasonality with plating. The bowl lip usually becomes thinner as it gets hot, and in summer we use glass bowls. In winter we use thicker wooden lacquerware and plates with a heavy glaze.

How would you describe the presentation of classic *kaiseki*?

[NY] There were many types originally, but the *kaiseki* meal that is common now is *cha kaiseki*, from the time of tea master Sen no Rikyu. In other words, it was a way of presenting small servings of seasonal things to eat while drinking delicious tea, but now it is more for drinking sake. In a small tea room they think about how they can make people enjoy the space, so they will consider details like whether to include a camellia or not. It isn't to make something gorgeous, but to make people feel the seasons.

Even if we use large plates and impressive plating, what we are doing is basically very simple. The actual cooking takes on our heritage, even if the presentation is new. There is no point in just doing staid things, so we have our antennas up and we include new trends too.

A set of Japanese knives.

There are around 10,000 tableware pieces at Kozue. This soup lid has both cherries and maple leaves on it, so it can be used in both spring and autumn.

Where do these trends come from?

[NY]   They come from all over: the internet, and also our colleagues. There are trends that come from produce providers, as well. Like, with meat, the technology for husbandry is really advanced. So in the past it was Yonezawa, Matsutaka and Kobe – the big brands. But now, there is really delicious beef everywhere. The thing that makes the difference is the thoughtfulness of the producers.

There are five places I procure my fish: the fisheries at Hakodate, Kanazawa, Yaizu, Owase and Toyosu. Previously, you would get everything from Toyosu central market. Now, local fisheries are really trying hard. In the past, these peripheral ports couldn't communicate with us directly and had to go through Toyosu, but there was a revision in the law in the last 10 years, so I can make local orders. Rather than making faceless transactions, Kozue is really working with fishermen who are thinking about which fish to send to us.

This tuna is from Mie, but we can't get that every day – the fishermen texted me last night and sent me a photo. Same with Yaizu – they are thinking about me and Kozue, and choose the ingredients. It is spontaneous. These kinds of processes are our secret weapon. In fact, it isn't just a trend; this kind of communication and these sorts of relationships are necessities nowadays. Through human connections we get information as well.

Chef Yoshida procures fish from local fisheries with whom he has a close relationship.

There is one man who goes into the mountains in Akita to get wild vegetables. I have no idea what kind of herbs or mushrooms will turn up, and he asks me not to make a specific order. I just ask him to get 5 kilograms (11 lb) of wild vegetables: three types, and three types of mushrooms. When I get them I am like, 'What is this?', and after sampling them, I decide what to make. There is a sense of interaction and stimulation; I will get a message in the middle of the night from Kanazawa, and then at 5 a.m. there will be one from Hakodate, then at 7 a.m. from Yanaizu. It is really enjoyable. Even in this modern skyscraper in Shinjuku, I will get messages like, 'The waves are so high in Yaizu that it is hard to take the ships out.' We want to express these real interactions at Kozue. I make an order the night before. And then the next morning, the produce arrives. Even from Hakodate, the ingredients go on the *shinkansen* in the morning and arrive at ours that night.

Buddhist Tofu Cuisine

Kadohama Goma-tofu honpo is a sesame tofu company based on the holy site of Mt Koya in central Japan. It aims to encourage people to enjoy their product, a type of health food for monks with a history that is over 1,200 years long. Sesame tofu contains protein that is often lacking in standard vegetarian and vegan *shojin ryori* (Buddhist) meals, so Kadohama aims to make the act of eating this kind of food both healthy and accessible. The dishes served in their restaurant employ what are said to be the most important elements within Japanese cuisine: five colours, five taste experiences and five cooking methods.

Koji Kadohama, CEO, Kadohama Goma-tofu honpo

What are the characteristics of sesame tofu?
[KK]   Koyasan sesame tofu was originally a type of health food, so we really take the health aspect seriously. The kanji (character) for *taberu* (to eat) is made up of the characters for 'good' and 'people'. The two ingredients are organic sesame and Yoshino *kuzu*, which is a starch from Yoshino that has warming properties; it is like Chinese medicine.
    The white sesame is organic. It is from a village in Myanmar. We peel the outside and use the interior only, so we use quite a few seeds – for a 5 cm x 5 cm (2 x 2 in.) piece of tofu, we use about 5,600 sesame seeds. During Covid we had no visitors, so I had time and I counted them.

Why are visuals so important in Japanese food?

[KK]   It is the aesthetics of the *goshiki* (five colours) that encapsulate the five flavours and the five aromas. One way to enjoy food is through the plating and the arrangement, so we made our meals into mandalas. There are two mandalas that Mt Koya Buddhist culture takes into account, the *taizokai* and the *kongokai* mandala: when you are eating your meal you can feel these mandalas slightly. We collaborate with lacquer artisans and we make these dishes to order. The best thing is that it is delicious as well; it is aesthetic and healthy.

How many artisans work with you?

[KK]   In total there are twenty, and it takes three years to become skilled. Only the people within the Kadohama company can do the last parts, which are the most important elements, where we mix the Yoshino *kuzu* and the sesame. It is something you do with the senses. We don't have written text instructions, it is only word-of-mouth, so the training takes a long time.

In Koyasan there are many aspects that are word-of-mouth only, such as the training for senior priests. It is a characteristic of *mikkyo* or Esoteric Buddhism, the Buddhism practised here. There are many of these kinds of secrets.

How do you express seasonality?

[KK]   Koyasan Buddhist food is usually split into three parts: *honzen*, *ninozen* and *sannozen*. The seasonal foods are placed in the *ninozen* and *sannozen* courses, and these include things like chestnuts during autumn.

What kind of place is Mt Koya?

[KK]   Kobo Daishi, the founder of Esoteric Buddhism, established it. It was originally a place of training. All the monks in Japan would go there to train. The Buddhist sect here is Shingon Esoteric Buddhism, which places emphasis on facing oneself, and deliberation and contemplation. Other sects often focus on praying to a god for help, but Shingon is more about finding a god within yourself. When we make sesame, to grind it is really difficult. The more you grind it, the more beneficial and easy to digest it is. It is like training.

Up until 150 years ago, there were only temples here. There are now 117 temples in the area and they all connect to make one large temple – this whole mountain of Koyasan is one large temple. We feel as though we are living within a temple precinct.

Kadohama says sesame tofu is part of Koyasan culture.

KOPPE BREAD BAKERY

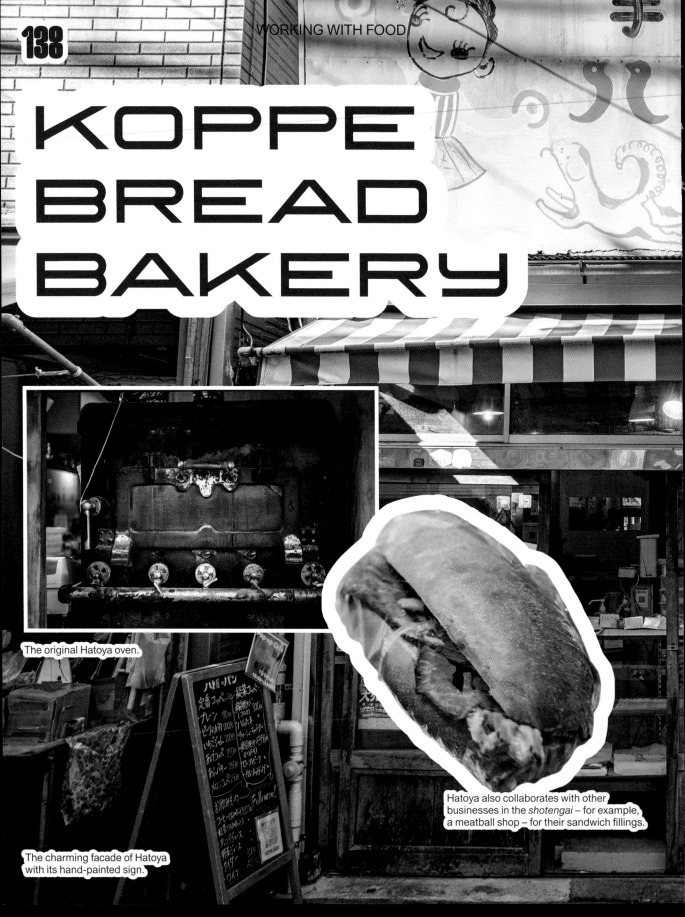

The original Hatoya oven.

The charming facade of Hatoya with its hand-painted sign.

Hatoya also collaborates with other businesses in the *shotengai* – for example, a meatball shop – for their sandwich fillings.

It's rare for a bakery to make only one type of bread.

Hatoya is a bakery on a Kyojima *shotengai* shopping street (see page 140) in Tokyo that specializes in *koppe* bread, which is taken from the French word 'coupe' (cut), as the bread is sliced down the centre. The bakery is known for creating a type of sandwich crammed with a variety of fillings, from sweet bean paste and butter to meatballs. Hatoya was established in 1912 (when bread was still quite unusual) and is a third-generation business. It exists in a type of area that is rare, since it wasn't firebombed during World War II.

Sakai, the baker at Hatoya, is a journalist. When covering sports, he often wrote about sumo wrestling, which brought him to the downtown Sumida region (of which Kyojima is part), known for its traditional culture. After Hatoya shuttered in 2017, in order to protect it from being demolished and turned into apartments, the owner, an urbanist with whom Sakai collaborates, bought the shop and restarted the business.

'We wanted to make it a place for the community to gather, so we made it so you can sit inside as opposed to a takeaway format,' Sakai says. 'There are more shops closing in the *shotengai*, but we want everyone to survive together. So we collaborate on items such as the *shotengai* sandwich, which has hamburger patties from another local shop. The *shotengai* is a lifestyle.'

He says the appeal of Hatoya is the fact that it doesn't change. 'Lots of people come in and are pleased that it is still here,' Sakai explains. 'People find that heart-warming.'

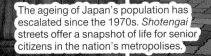

The ageing of Japan's population has escalated since the 1970s. *Shotengai* streets offer a snapshot of life for senior citizens in the nation's metropolises.

SHOTENGAI

A common feature of downtown districts in Japan is the *shotengai*, a linear shopping street filled with grocery stores, cafés, tofu shops, barbers and fishmongers. There are an estimated 15,000 of them across the nation, and they generally sport cheerful names like Joyful Minowa. Each shop is usually highly specialized, quite often serving only one type of food, such as *takoyaki* octopus balls or pickles – and because of this, their products are of artisanal quality. The owners frequently have close relationships with elderly shoppers.

These *shotengai*-orientated areas have been a part of metropolises in Japan since the 1500s. However, like many aspects of downtown urbanism, they have been under steady decline for close to two decades, facing competition from supermarkets and large shopping centres. *Shotengai* such as Tsuruhashi in Osaka and Ameyoko in Ueno also have high concentrations of shops run by ethnic minorities (Korean for the former and Chinese for the latter), and are still one of the best places to source rare ingredients.

Shotengai are a good place to obtain spices and sauces not available anywhere else in Japan.

Ueno's Ameyoko *shotengai* is at the site of a former post-war black market. Besides food, it's home to a number of sneaker shops, shops selling *ska-jan* embroidered jackets and leather manufacturers.

Ameyoko *shotengai* is packed with many Chinese food street stalls.

Residents in the area are often proactive in maintaining the neighbourhood on a grassroots level.

Lee Chapman

Junko Mizuno

NELSON WU

SAEBORG

Osamu Watanabe

Pobot

Maya Fuji

ART

Junko Mizuno

The Last Course: Ouroboros,
2022, acrylic on wood panel.

Ambrosial Affair: Eggs, 2015, acrylic on canvas.

Junko Mizuno is a Japanese artist currently residing in San Francisco, California. Her striking, often erotic pieces feature strong women rendered in retro *kawaii* pastel hues. She works in a number of mediums, from painting to illustration to designer toys. Influenced by a wide-ranging array of lowbrow sources such as fetish and psychedelic art, vintage art and folk iconography, Mizuno's work is sexy and dynamic.

The Last Course: Meat, 2022, acrylic on wood panel.

Ambrosial Affair: Pomegranate, 2015,
acrylic on canvas.

Besides powerful women, her art often features food such as eggs, fruit and noodles. As Mizuno explains, 'I basically draw food just because it's fun, but I like the fact that food in art can be seen as a symbol of life, energy and joy. I love that there are so many different kinds of food with different shapes and colours. Ever since I can remember, I've been obsessed with food. As a child, I was excited when I found food images in books. I loved drawing and making food out of paper or clay. I grew up in Japan, where women were supposed to be cute, shy and graceful. I was always frustrated with that idea, and I think that's one of the reasons I love depicting powerful, greedy, hungry women devouring food without caring how other people think about them at all.'

Mizuno admits that, because she works from home and rarely meets up with people, eating is the most exciting thing in her everyday life: 'It gives me energy and, of course, inspiration for my art.'

Ambrosial Affair: Noodle, 2015, acrylic on canvas.

The Last Course: Rice, 2022, acrylic on wood panel.

Osamu Watanabe

Sweets Kamakura, 2023, modelling paste, resin, styrene foam, fibre-reinforced plastic (FRP).

Osamu Watanabe is a self-proclaimed 'sweets artist' who makes decorative sculptures using resin. His often fantastical and romantic statues, made in the likeness of unicorns, Pegasuses and swans, are adorned with a mind-boggling array of fake cream, cake toppings, puddings and other embellishments.

Watanabe takes inspiration from the actual sweets that he enjoys eating, but makes the colours more vibrant and vivid, so they are easy to associate with childhood memories. He has seen the artistry associated with sweets up close since he was a child, since his mother is a sweets chef. He started making sweets-inspired art in college in the early 2000s.

Osamu Watanabe, sweets artist, sculptor

What inspires your art?
[OW] I am influenced by Impressionism and
nihonga (classic Japanese painting). I look at
old work, rather than contemporary work. I am
inspired by actual real sweets; for instance,
the colourways are from existing food. Every
year the trends change, as there are numerous
satellite patisserie shops in Tokyo from top
international chefs. Even without going
overseas, I can try first-class sweets.

  Because of these trends, sweets from
all over the world get combined with local food,
especially in Tokyo. For example, *maritozzo*
(a cream-filled bun) is from Italy, but rather
than being authentic, it is mixed with *dorayaki*
(a sweet bean pancake) and turned into an
original product. I think Japan is good at
morphing things from abroad; another example
is *castella* (a type of honey cake), which is
originally from Portugal, but has now become
a kind of Japanese shortcake.

Fountain of Sweets, 2023, modelling
paste, resin, FRP, mirror sheet.

Sweet and Fleeting City of Sweets, 2023,
modelling paste, resin, ceramic, FRP.

Why are Western sweets so popular in *kawaii* culture?

[OW]   In the Heian period, the notion of *kawaii* was described in the books *The Pillow Book* and *The Tale of Genji*. There are minute descriptions of sensual beauty and cute things, so I think there have been these kinds of sensibilities within the culture for a long time. Even adults will carry cute things. However, the roots of sweets are European. I think it is the colours; they suit *kawaii* culture. Sweet things are addictive and captivating.

What are the main themes in your work?

[OW]   I'm trying to express a 'sweets utopia'. There is a lot of dark news out there these days, yet I am working in the art world, so I want to make something bright and uplifting by contrast. There is also the suggestion that utopia doesn't exist, so I'm working with the notion of making your own utopia. I think that the more stressful the world is, the less you might feel up to looking at artworks with acute political messages. Japan is economically stressed, so I want the artwork at least to be fantastical.

Sweets Merry-Go-Round, 2023, modelling paste, resin, FRP, iron.

Supper of Sweets, 2023, modelling paste, resin, ceramic, FRP, mirror sheet, wood.

I'm Thinking, 2017, modelling paste, resin, FRP.

NELSON WU

Conbini are a ubiquitous feature of any Japanese town or city. Vending machines and air conditioners regularly feature in Nelson Wu's work.

Nelson Wu is a pixel artist and illustrator based in Toronto, Canada, who works in the game and entertainment industry. He also sells his work online and at conventions. Wu's series on convenience stores is an homage to the more than 50,000 *conbini* that are found in almost every town and city in Japan, such as 7/11, Family Mart and Lawsons. They live up to their name, offering a wide array of products, 24/7 service and high-quality hot and cold food that is aligned with the seasons. Wu often buys products at *conbini* for packaging design research, as the seasonal offerings rotate at a pace that reflects current food trends.

Nelson Wu, artist

What exactly is pixel art?
[NW]   Pixel art is a medium born from the early stages of computers and video games. There were only a limited amount of pixels to work with back then, creating a very distinct style both in terms of dimensions and the number of colours. The goal of pixel art is to depict your subject matter within the limitations given. A lot of iconic video games were created in pixel art that influenced an entire generation of players: titles such as *Space Invaders* (1978), *Pac-Man* (1980) and *Super Mario Bros.* (1985), to name a few. Having said that, pixel art has had a resurgence of popularity in modern video games, animations and artwork online, and it is celebrated widely. The tools artists have today are much more advanced than 40 years ago; pixel art can be taken a lot further as a medium and creators can take many more artistic liberties.

It is not an over-exaggeration to suggest that a person can live off *conbini* food.

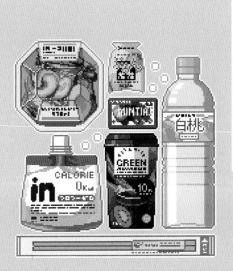

Typical offerings include rice balls, bento boxes, sweets and drinks.

What is the process of making pixel art like?
[NW]   There's a lot within the process, but it starts with defining my constraints. Canvas size really determines how my pixel art comes out. After that, it's all about depicting my subject matter within these constraints. I come from an illustration background so I treat it like painting, starting with a rough sketch, colour fill and rendering.

Why do you think *conbini* became so popular in Japan?
[NW]   They're safe, convenient and accessible to everyone. They've become a part of everyday life. A lot of it has to do with urban planning and differences in lifestyle. Everything is within walking or biking distance, or near public transit. On the other hand, North America is mostly a car-centric suburbia where people drive to supermarkets and big box stores, apart from the cities' cores.

What are your favourite *conbini* foods?
[NW]   My favourite things to get at a *conbini* are the *onigiri* rice balls. Salmon, spicy *mentaiko* and on rare occasions *ikura* if it's available! I also really like their chip and drink selection, since there's always a new flavour I haven't tried before. I love getting any type of green or oolong tea or Pocari Sweat (a type of sugary sports drink) for a long walk. Chu-hi's are really great too; they are alcoholic fruity sodas that are unique to Japan.

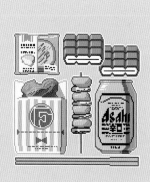
Wu is attracted to the variety of items on offer at *conbini*.

Wu travels to Asia, Hong Kong, Japan and Taiwan often, and is drawn to the architecture and urban planning of these regions.

Wu says, 'I tend to gravitate towards
quiet slice-of-life moments.'

Lee Chapman

Lee Chapman is a British documentary and street photographer and long-term resident of Japan who is known for his candid images of Tokyo. He captures natural and spontaneous moments, and although his shots are unposed, he tries to convey stories of the places that embody the true charm of the city. His photos of downtown eateries are particularly evocative: small, intimate spaces that provide respite, familiarity and warmth in a metropolis of over 13.5 million people. Chapman's photos show the brief moments and encounters that these small establishments catalyse, reflecting the human desire for community, gathering, communication and interaction – all while enjoying a simple and heartfelt meal.

Photographer Lee Chapman is known for finding the best hygono eateries in Tokyo. These intimate spaces provide warmth and intimacy in a giant city.

Lee Chapman, photographer

You shoot a lot in unknown places around Tokyo. How do you find them?

[LC]   It's basically been lots of walking over many years. The vast majority of those meanders have been on the side streets, where, for me at least, life is and also looks more interesting.

Taito and Sumida wards are by far my favourite areas to walk and photograph in, and if I had to pick one neighbourhood, it'd probably be Kyojima. There's always so much to see and enjoy in regards to both people and places. In an odd way, its old-school vibe also gives me what I can only describe as nostalgia by proxy, as I barely experienced life here last century – let alone in Showa-era Japan.

What draws you to an establishment?

[LC]   Anywhere that is small, old and unpretentious is always a good start, and if it's somewhat on the ramshackle and grubby side, then even better. Essentially, somewhere that has barely changed over the years and seems like its stained walls contain countless untold stories.

The proprietors of these eateries are one of the main reasons people return to these spaces.

People are not strangers for long in these tiny spaces. The physical proximity and laid-back atmosphere allow conversation to flow easily.

Yakitori is one of the simple foods found at classic eateries.

Your work features charming protagonists – who have a resilience and strength to survive – and their businesses. How would you describe the people in your photos?

[LC]   Resilience is always a factor. To run a bar or restaurant for decades and continue doing so well past retirement age needs that as a bare minimum. Then, there's also a sense of commitment, duty and often simply the habit of always having done so. It is, in many ways, just what they do, and also in a very real sense who they are.

It's probably true to say they are also different from the majority of citizens. They are people who have made their own way in life on their own terms; firmly and resolutely rejecting the corporate and salaried world that so many of their generation, and indeed subsequent ones, have wholeheartedly embraced.

What function do the small eateries you shoot have in a city like Tokyo?

[LC]   They are second homes where people can relax after work, or at the weekend. Places where, if they want to, they can chat with other locals and the owner, or just enjoy being with other people. Despite its many millions of residents, Tokyo can be a lonely city, often with little or no interaction between neighbours. Plus, offices and the like are invariably all about work, not personal relationships or connections. So in that sense, these little bars and eateries can provide a much-needed sense of belonging and the simple pleasure of being looked after by the mama or master-san.

These spaces are accessible and friendly, even for people eating on their own. They provide a community atmosphere which brings regulars back time and again.

Can you describe the dynamic between yourself and your subjects?

[LC]   It depends on the situation. As an obvious foreigner in such places, it's impossible to simply spend a few hours eating and drinking and just blend in. On entering, there's invariably a bit of a fuss and a flurry of questions. All that breaks the ice though, and so once I'm settled in, it's much easier to bring the camera out and take a few photos.

In less than spacious surroundings, it really is essential that people are comfortable with both me and, later on, the camera. Those initial questions help provide all those present with some understanding of why I chose that particular place, a bit of a backstory, and, perhaps more importantly, the reassurance that I'm there primarily to enjoy the food, ambience and surroundings just like they are.

All that combines to make taking photos both easy and natural. There's no need for poses or permission. Basically, I become another customer – one who just happens to be foreign and also has a camera.

What's your favourite photo that you've taken at a food-related establishment?

[LC]   If I had to choose one, it'd be of this 93-year-old bar owner in Tokyo's far west, pictured here. Her little place ticked most of those boxes I mentioned earlier, and remains the only bar I've been to run by someone in their 90s. She was also absolutely lovely. Someone who was happy to sit there and listen to the radio when there were no customers, and similarly happy to serve and cook if there were. All the while sipping on hot sake. The stories she told us about being displaced when a nearby dam was built, and riding on a now long-abandoned old cable car in the area, were truly fascinating. A very different world and life.

It was also the one and only time I visited. I returned a couple of times, but I was either too early, too late, or it was her day off. Then, a year or so later, I found out she had died. A sad inevitability, and unfortunately the way many of these places go. It's an important reminder to make the most of them, and their owners, while they are still here.

One of Chapman's favourite shots, of a
93-year-old owner of an old-school eatery.

Pobot

Pobot makes ultra-cute clay figurines based on a variety of Japanese food, like these cat-shaped hamburgers.

Pobot is a clay artist who makes adorable, pastel-coloured miniature sweets that are often combined with animal motifs. Her work also reflects the annual change in seasons – she uses themes such as flowers that bloom in the rainy season, as well as seasonal traditional foods. Pobot has garnered a massive following on social media. She explains, 'I hope to express Japanese aesthetic cuteness in my own way, using motifs like mochi and *dorayaki*. In particular, I think mochi is a food with a unique texture, so I place importance on how I can express this in a cute way with clay. I would be happy if you could be comforted by the mochi's round shape!'

Shiba Inu-themed *anko* bread, a type of bread with sweet bean filling.

ぽぽっと。

All of Pobot's clay pieces look like edible delights.

A clay creation referencing a *sakura* mochi sweet.

Set of clay macarons with Shiba filling.

Of her impetus to start making things with clay, she says, 'I loved dollhouses and miniatures as a child, but many of them were expensive. I could not afford to buy them, so I started making what I wanted. Gradually, I began to receive feedback on the works I was making, and I started selling my works when I was in high school as I had no allowance.'

Pobot explains that the appeal of clay is the tactile sensation she gets when making things, which she finds soothing, as well as the ability to create freely: 'You can craft the shape you want to make with clay in a three-dimensional form, and shapes that are difficult to reproduce with food are possible with clay.'

Pobot says that new designs usually come to her when she is mindlessly working with clay: 'From there, I form what comes to mind and make a sample, and if I like it, I start the main production.'

Shiba Inu-themed melon bread figures.

SAEBORG

Saeborg's work is livestock-themed as a way to explore the concept of vulnerability.

Saeborg is a Tokyo-based performance artist who describes herself as an 'imperfect cyborg'. She wears flamboyant inflatable latex outfits that she's crafted herself in order to transform into various personas, transcending fixed categories like gender and species.

A concept that Saeborg has long explored in her work is that of livestock and slaughterhouse animals as signifiers of vulnerability and weakness. While looking at multispecies coexistence and animal consumption, she presents these themes as incongruously colourful and fantastical worlds, via inflatable and playful domesticated animal characters.

She started out performing at Tokyo's underground clubs (such as Department H), which she continues to do today, but also exhibits at major art festivals and museums across the world. Saeborg was the recipient of the Tokyo Contemporary Art Award in 2022.

Saeborg, artist

What is the appeal of latex as a medium?
[S]   The fit when you wear it. It is inflatable, and you can change your body and transform accordingly. I really like masks, and things that you wear on your face. I started to get them made to order from latex designers such as Kurage in Ikebukuro. After that, I began to make them on my own. Latex is a weak material. It degrades, but I like that about it.

How did you get into latex in the first place?
[S]   I like drag queens, and there is a film that I like called *Vegas in Space*, with these gorgeous queens on what looks like a cheap S&M set. It is really fun. The mistress that appears in it has what looks like drag queen makeup, but actually it's a mask. I found that impressive, and realized that if it's a mask, you can change it easily. I tried all kinds of masks, like *bishojo kigurumi* [a full face in the likeness of a beautiful girl], as that was in at the time in Japan.

Pigpen, 2016, performance at Department-H at TOKYO KINEMA CLUB. Saeborg says that, as an art school graduate, making her own latex outfits was a trial-and-error process.

Saeborg also likes that latex needs a lot of care and maintenance. She think it's like a pet, and the relationship with a particular item can continue over time.

Saeborg with friends at Department-H. To create her pieces, she first makes a figure of herself sculpturally, then makes a mould based on that so she can design an outfit to her size and make a pattern.

Have you been using domesticated animal themes since the beginning?

[S]   When I was doing experimental work, I was making things like aliens. But since I started exhibiting, it has been domesticated animal themes. I made a cow and then decided to make this into a series.

A lot of people ask whether I am vegan and into animal rights, but actually I am interested in weak things – and when you're thinking about vulnerability, it is easy to think of domesticated animals. But I would research these issues, and if I got a commission from a prefecture (for example, a museum invite), I would ask them to arrange a viewing of the local processing plants. If I asked a slaughterhouse on my own, they would refuse.

There were a few times when an abattoir was quite different to what I imagined. The narrative is usually about animal abuse, but it was quite different when I saw it. People generally imagine the slaughter, but there is an extremely long process; the culling is only a moment. The animal is kept for a long time prior to that – actually, I am more interested in that.

Are you interested in identity transformation?

[S]   Yes, you can become what you want to. And you can change your shape. With something like tattoos, you can remove them, but it is quite difficult. But with latex, you can change it freely. I can design my corporeal self, and all my characters have names. They are all extensions of myself and I can expand selfhood indefinitely. I can create my own avatar in bulk.

Do you think that animism impacts views on multispecies interactions in Japan?
[S]   There is the notion of 8 million gods [an animistic view that everything has a life] in Shinto, and there are souls in everything, including inanimate things. At the moment, the term 'eco' is in fashion, but in Japan the concept of *mottainai* (not wasting things) has existed since long ago. There is the notion that one must coexist with nature, even if it is tough on humans. Instead of taking revenge, there is a necessity to live in harmony with nature, rather than the conception that nature is evil and should be destroyed.

Do you use anthropomorphic animals, or animals 'as-is'?
[S]   It is a mix. I want to make something that isn't human, but the design has to be something I can wear. But actually, the fewer human elements there are, the more interesting it is. Although, if you remove all the human elements, then it's not interesting either.

Department H is where Saeborg first performed from 2010 to 2015 at rubber events. Even though she now participates in the world's most prestigious art festivals, she still stays true to her underground roots and is a regular here.

Saeborg set out to make large artworks – but rather than, for example, creating a monumental bronze statue, she was attracted to latex suits that she can wear.

Maya Fuji

A Post Bath Treat, 2022, acrylic on wood panel.

Maya Fuji is a first-generation mixed-race Japanese American artist who uses food in her work as a means to connect with her heritage. Her vibrant pieces feature voluptuous women who are comfortable with their bodies; many of her scenes depict them eating and sharing food in intimate settings, such as at family gatherings and bathhouses. Fuji explores the history of Japanese cuisine and its cultural relevance in her art. For her, food symbolizes community, tradition and spirituality.

Maya Fuji, artist

Please explain your background, in terms of food.
[MF]   Being raised in the Bay Area, I grew up eating a whole range of foods from many different cultures. Because I moved to the US at a very young age, I didn't necessarily have culture shock, but I definitely stood out during school lunches when I would show up with my bento boxes. Kids used to ask me to trade their Fruit Roll-Up for my 'sushi' (which was in fact *onigiri* rice balls). At home, our dinner spread would usually consist of staples like miso soup and *hiyayakko* (chilled tofu), but we'd also have more American mains like pork chops lining the table as well. My favourite was Japanese breakfast, with dishes like grilled *sanma* (saury) pickles, rice, *natto* and miso soup!

Eating Crab at Country Station, 2022, acrylic on wood panel.

Eating Crab at Country Station (Close Up), 2022, acrylic on wood panel.

What kinds of values does food symbolize in your work?

[MF]   Food symbolizes many things for me, including community, tradition, storytelling, love language and health. It has been a big part of my life because I've worked in the restaurant industry, mostly at Japanese restaurants, for the majority of my adult life. I've had the pleasure of working with a Michelin-level *kaiseki* chef who was classically trained in the Kyoto style, and learned a lot about the history and seasonality of the dishes.

      The attention to detail used to pair specific ceramic tableware with each course, and how each dish is meticulously and artfully plated, has always fascinated me. I think the long history of what these dishes represent is an essential part of Japanese culture, and is a method which I've stayed connected to. I've noticed that, oftentimes, when a certain ingredient is mentioned, a lot of Japanese people know what region of Japan is famous for it, what season is best to enjoy it in and what its health benefits are. I feel like this creates a sense of pride in the cuisine and the regional cultures of Japan.

      One of my love languages is to lure friends to my house and cook for them. Sharing food over stories is probably one of my favourite pastimes.

When you use Japanese food in your art, what are your references?

[MF]   I am fascinated by the artful detail that goes into *kaiseki*. I often work with themes of tradition, mythology and cultural significance, and I think these themes permeate the thought and care that go into creating a *kaiseki* menu. I also reference regional specialities from Kanazawa (my hometown in Ishikawa prefecture), because we are known for having some of the best cuisine in Japan!

Midnight Snack, 2022, acrylic on wood panel.

What is the link between food and your Japanese and American identities in your work?

[MF]   Because I spent much of my childhood going back and forth between both countries, I found there was an ebb and flow to each side of my identity. At times, I would feel more comfortable with my Japanese side, but it did conflict with the pressure to also assimilate into American culture. Food has definitely been a way for me to stay connected to my Japanese identity, and at home I almost exclusively cook Japanese food. It has been one of the links that have kept my language skills and knowledge of Japan at the level that they are at today.

A Midnight Feast, 2022, acrylic and
rhinestone on wood panel.

PICTURE CREDITS

ABOUT THE AUTHOR

Manami Okazaki is a journalist and researcher based in Japan. She has authored 13 books on Japanese culture, including *Kawaii! Japan's Culture of Cute*, *Kimono Now*, *Land of the Rising Cat: Japan's Feline Fascination* and *Japan's Best Friend: Dog Culture in the Land of the Rising Sun* (all published by Prestel). Her journalism has been featured in the *Japan Times*, *Wall Street Journal*, *South China Morning Post*, *Guardian*, *Lonely Planet*, *Transit* and other global media outlets. She is also a curator of Japanese folk craft exhibitions across the world.

© Aziz Tnani

ACKNOWLEDGEMENTS

Thanks to my editors Ali Gitlow and Martha Jay, designers Nina Jua Klein and John Philip Sage, and Andrew Hansen at Prestel. Professor Lynne Nakano, Professor Venera Khalikova and Professor Isaac Gagne at CUHK for introducing me to anthropology. Tomoko Kirino, Yoshimoto Itoh at San-x, everyone in the Kyojima neighborhood (especially Ayumu Haitani at Muumuu), Kaela Jade Mitchell at Masa Designs, Sota Suzuki at Torture Garden Japan, Gogh *Imaizumi* at Department H, Aya Sato, Keiko Hamae at Park Hyatt Tokyo, Yuka Kraft, Yurie Suzuki, Aiko Ueno and Minako Hayata at Aman Tokyo, Hideaki Tanaka and Mr Sasamoto at Being, Rin Rin, Sekiya Takumi, Oishi Shohei and Sakamoto Shunta at Bento Architecture Design Office, Yuta Watanabe at Izu Mentaiko Park, Moe Asakura and Yuji Takano at Namja Town, Hiroko Nakamura at the Kyoto Manga Museum, Mr Chiba at 90884, Takashi Nakai at Ganso Sample, Iwasaki, Kurebayashi and everyone who ate food with me while making this book.

© Prestel Verlag,
Munich · London · New York, 2024
A member of Penguin Random House
Verlagsgruppe GmbH
Neumarkter Strasse 28 · 81673 Munich

© for the text by Manami Okazaki, 2024
© for the photographs see Picture Credits,
p. 174, 2024

Library of Congress Control Number:
2023944557

A CIP catalogue record for this book is available
from the British Library.

Editorial direction: Ali Gitlow
Copyediting and proofreading: Martha Jay
Design and layout: Nina Jua Klein and
John Philip Sage
Production management: Luisa Klose
Separations: Reproline Mediateam, Munich
Printing and binding: DZS Grafik, Slovenia
Paper: Magno Volume FSC

FSC
www.fsc.org

MIX
Paper | Supporting
responsible forestry
FSC® C106600

Penguin Random House Verlagsgruppe
FSC® N001967

Printed in Slovenia

ISBN 978-3-7913-8923-3

www.prestel.com